HOLDING SERVE

PERSEVERING ON *and* OFF *the* COURT

———— • ————

MICHAEL CHANG
with MIKE YORKEY

REGENCY PUBLISHING HOUSE
NASHVILLE / NEW YORK

Published in Nashville, Tennessee, by Thomas Nelson, Inc.

All Scriptures used are from the HOLY BIBLE: NEW INTERNATIONAL VERSION®. Copyright © 1973, 1978, 1984 by International Bible Society. Used by permission of Zondervan Publishing House. All rights reserved.

Library of Congress Cataloging-in-Publication Data

Chang, Michael, 1972–
    Holding serve / Michael Chang.
        p. cm.
    ISBN 0-7852-8822-8
    1. Chang, Michael, 1972– 2. Tennis players—United States—Biography.
3. Christian biography—United States. I. Title.

GV994.C47 C42 2002
796.342'092—dc21
[B]   2001056225

Printed in the United States of America
02 03 04 05 06 BVG 5 4 3 2 1

To my father and mother, Joe and Betty Chang

———— • ————

Without you, none of this would have been possible.
Thank you for your unconditional love and support.

CONTENTS

INTRODUCTION

This book is a long time coming.

I think it is because the first time someone asked me whether I would write a book, thirty minutes had passed since I won the French Open in 1989.

I exaggerate, of course, but the fame of becoming the youngest male to win a Grand Slam tournament caused many in the media—and tennis fans around the world—to wonder if a book by me would be forthcoming. Since winning the French Open, I have received numerous offers from book publishing companies asking me to tell my story. I turned them all down. I never thought the time was right until now, which calls for an explanation.

An autobiography is supposed to sum up the thoughts of someone who has made history or has been in the limelight for some reason. Since I have turned thirty years of age, I have forty-five years waiting in front of me, if God grants me an average life expectancy. It would be ludicrous for me to summarize my life at this time. After all, I have a lot of life left to live.

Nonetheless, I realize that I have only a couple of seasons—if God grants me those years—remaining in the game. Thus, with the next phase of life just ahead, I feel it is important to record my thoughts and observations before I exit the playground of professional tennis. You can call *Holding Serve* a midterm reflection.

Besides, a book about me at the age of seventeen would have been pretty boring. Sure, I had a wonderful upbringing, but most of my days from first grade on were spent in school or on a tennis court, hitting a fuzzy yellow ball. The life of a tennis professional is rather one-dimensional: we all stay in the same hotels (generally), wake up, eat breakfast, call the transportation desk for a ride to the tournament site, loosen up in the locker room before warming up for a half hour or so, and then play our matches. Afterward, there are postmatch interviews, people to meet, and trainers to visit. Then it is back to the hotel room for a meal and some rest—or to the airport, if we failed to win the last point of the match. A jet flight takes off for the next tour stop, or home sweet home for one of our infrequent respites from the tour.

In *Holding Serve* I will recount my tennis career to this point, making sure I touch on the highlights and lowlights, but I will also tell you more about myself than you've read elsewhere. I have done thousands of interviews over the years, but my questioners often failed to ask me what was *really* important in life. Besides, no matter what I said, the scribes usually wrote what they wanted to anyway. Some got it right, but more often than not, the pictures they painted of me were incomplete.

You see, I am a Christian. You've probably heard me thank the Lord in a postmatch interview and give Him the glory. That's who I am and who I will be long after I step away from the game. In this book, I'll explain what my faith means to me and how I have learned that life is more than cheering crowds or TV interviews or department store appearances or even triumphant victories. I have lived half my life sold-out to Jesus Christ, and I shudder to think how I could have gotten through the past fifteen years without His guidance and love.

God has a plan for my life, just as He has one for you. If you will stick with me on the following pages, you will learn more about that plan and how much I look forward to the next chapter of my life. Thanks for joining me.

• FRENCH OPEN, JUNE 1989 •

·

CHAPTER I

SPRINGTIME IN PARIS

If there is one common denominator to the gypsy lives led by tennis
players, it is jet lag. I wouldn't go so far as to call jet lag an occupa-
tional hazard, but upon return to my home on Mercer Island (a Seattle
suburb), I don't force my weary body—or my restless mind—to sleep
until the sun comes up. I like to bring my body clock around more naturally, which means that if I awaken at 2 A.M.—my mind fully alert and
my body somewhat rested—I get out of bed.

When that happens, I throw on a sweatshirt, a pair of jeans, and
some old tennis shoes and step out onto the balcony of my lakefront
home, which overlooks the western shoreline of Mercer Island. To the
north, I can see the white glow of headlights from eastbound travelers
riding I-90's floating bridge, the six-lane ribbon of concrete that con-
nects Mercer Island to Seattle to the west and Bellevue to the east.

Lake Washington is very still, given the hour. The ink-black water is
glassy smooth; beads of lights up and down the coastline shimmer
upon the lake's surface. At this time—the dead of night, when the

1

world outside my home is fast asleep but I'm not—I walk to my dock and step into my nineteen-foot Ranger walleye bass boat with my G. Loomis fishing rod in hand. I motor up to my favorite fishing spot—a place near the I-90 bridge, about five minutes from home. I cut the engine and drop a line into the water while I drink in the quiet and peacefulness.

I look to the star-filled sky and remember that "the heavens declare the glory of God; the skies proclaim the work of his hands," as Psalm 19:1 says. Amid the beauty and stillness of the night, I turn reflective. Then I recall an event that turned a boy into a man, all in the span of two weeks in the City of Light—Paris, France.

THE EARLY ROUNDS AT ROLAND GARROS

I was seventeen years, three months, and seven days old when the French Open—the world's premier clay court tournament held over a two-week period—began welcoming tennis fans from around the world on Monday, May 30, 1989. The *Championats International de France* is played at a venue called Roland Garros, located in the Bois du Boulogne, a tree-lined park in the western suburbs of Paris. The French constructed the art deco tennis complex in 1928 to host France's Davis Cup defense against the United States and named it after Roland Garros, a World War I flying ace. During my first French Open in 1988, I learned that the French say *Ro-lahnd Garrow,* while Americans mistakenly add the *s* sound.

I was the eighteenth-ranked player in the world when the French Open began, but when John McEnroe, Emilio Sanchez, and Thomas Muster withdrew because of injuries, the tournament committee bumped me into the elite group of sixteen seeded players. (I was also one of four players seventeen and under—the others being Pete Sampras, Goran Ivanisevic, and Fabrice Santoro.)

Back then, Roland Garros was home to eighteen courts, all covered with a slippery surface called *terre battue*—literally "battered earth" or what we call red clay. The salmon-colored surface is made out of specially crushed bricks produced in the French village of Hermenon. Playing tennis on clay would be similar to playing tennis on the dirt portion of the Los Angeles Dodgers infield. The clay slows down the bounce of the ball considerably, so when a player hits a big serve or whacks a huge forehand, the ball loses substantial speed once it hits the ground. This changes tennis from a mindless "power game" to a greater mental test of patience, placements, endurance, and fortitude. You must learn to "slide" into your shots and keep your balance while moving about the court. If you're not used to clay, it can feel as if you are playing tennis on roller skates.

Although I had grown up in Southern California, where clay courts were few and far between, I liked playing on clay the infrequent times I got a chance to try it out. In the juniors, I played only two or three tournaments on the stuff. I found that clay suited my game, which was based on consistency and counterpunching, not blazing serves or big forehands. However, I had little clay court experience at age seventeen—a handful of weeks compared to the years of the veteran players.

In the late 1980s, Americans, if I can generalize, didn't like playing on clay because we grew up playing on hard courts. Shots that would be winners on faster surfaces were returned easily on clay. You could rip two or three shots into a corner only to have your crafty opponent float the ball back and make you hit that shot all over again. Net rushers found that their volleys sat up, so it was easier for their opponents to make passing shots. Clay, which caked to your socks, could get to your head if you didn't change your mind-set.

Roland Garros had become a red-earthed graveyard for American players. Going into the 1989 French Open, thirty-four years had passed since Tony Trabert had become the last American to conquer Roland Garros in 1955. Stan Smith and Arthur Ashe never came close. John McEnroe let a two-sets-to-love lead slip away against Ivan Lendl in the 1984 final and was handed probably the most frustrating loss of his career. Jimmy Connors reached four semifinals but could never quite get over the hump. Harold Solomon, Brian Gottfried, and Vitas Gerulaitis did earn spots in the finals, but the latter two lost one-sided matches in straight sets. Because Americans experienced such futility in Paris, Tony Trabert took phone calls every May from tennis writers asking him whether this was going to be the year that would end the American drought. Those annual interviews became a rite of spring for him, he said.

While Tony was fielding questions for another round of stories ("No Feats of Clay Foreseen in Paris" was a typical headline), I was training in Palm Springs, the Southern California desert resort community about a ninety-minute drive from my hometown of Placentia in Orange County. The Mission Hills Country Club in nearby Rancho Mirage had several clay courts and a great coach named José Higueras.

Each day I worked with José and another young tennis pro named Pete Sampras, who was six months older than I. Pete and I had been playing each other since we were eight years old, first squaring off at a tournament held at Poway High School in San Diego. Pete had a two-handed backhand in those days and was as steady as a backboard. The Southern California junior tennis world was a small universe, and Pete and I and a kid from Las Vegas named Andre Agassi seemed to run into each other at every tournament. Since Pete and I were closer in age, we grew up playing and practicing with each other—even playing doubles together for a spell. On many occasions when my mother, Betty, and I traveled to out-of-town tournaments, Pete hung out with us, which made sense. When you are in a new place, you naturally gravitate toward the people you know.

So it seemed natural that Pete and I would spend a couple of weeks training together at Mission Hills under the watchful eye of José Higueras, an accomplished Spanish player from the 1970s who knew clay court tennis. Pete had turned pro, as had I, and the United States Tennis Association (USTA) was paying our expenses under a Rookie Pro program. We stayed in a condo at a nearby Embassy Suites, and one day after training, Pete dropped by our room for a little conversation and some food. In those days, we were famished after training, and Pete knew where to go to satisfy his hunger pangs. Then again, kids are always hungry at age seventeen.

Pete smelled Mom's homemade spaghetti sauce simmering on the stove. I had always loved Mom's spaghetti sauce, filled with lean ground beef, fresh tomato sauce, and wonderful spices. Mom was a great cook, but we found out that Pete's tastes were different from ours.

"Pete, would you like to stay and have some fresh spaghetti with us?" Mom asked.

Pete didn't have to be asked twice. Mom returned to the kitchen to boil the water for the pasta.

Fifteen minutes later, lunch was ready. "Here you go, boys," said Mom.

"This tastes great, Mommy," I said as I dug in. I noticed that Pete wasn't eating. He had a question.

"Hey, Mrs. Chang, do you have any Ragu?"

"Ragu?" And then Mom understood. "Pete, that's home-made spaghetti sauce. Everything's fresh. It tastes very good."

"That's okay, Mrs. Chang. If it's all the same, I like the regular spaghetti sauce. Are you sure you don't have any Ragu?"

Meanwhile, Pete and I continued to train at Mission Hills. At the end of our daily workouts, I jogged for about an hour. Several times, I felt my legs cramping up. *That's strange,* I thought. *Why am I cramping?* I was in the best shape of my life, yet each time the painful cramps struck, I slowed to a standstill and walked back to the locker room. I told Mom and José, and we all agreed that the cramping was unusual for me.

One morning during a break, I was talking with José about the upcoming French Open. Paris seemed a million miles away.

"What do you think, José? Do I have a chance to win?" I asked earnestly.

It was an impertinent question, I now realize, a question that only a seventeen-year-old can ask, but at the time, I was serious.

"I think you might have a chance in the coming years, but probably not this year," José offered. Part of his job was not to dash the hopes of his charges. "Just keep working hard though."

"No, José, I mean this year. Why not this year?"

José let the question float in the air before saying, "I don't think you can realistically think about winning Roland Garros this year," he said. "But that's not the end of the world. You'll have your chance some year."

I had no reason to expect to win the French Open at the age of seventeen, but something within me sensed that something special would happen in Paris. I didn't know what it was, but a feeling of hope and expectation filled my heart. I returned to the practice court with a little extra spring to my step.

Unbeknownst to me, my mother had an interesting conversation with my father, Joe, right before the French Open started.

"This is really strange, but I have this feeling that Michael is going to win the French Open," said Mom.

"What?" he asked. Then he realized that Mom was not kidding. "Come on, really?"

"I'm serious."

"Well, that's an optimistic attitude," Dad remarked. He knew not to doubt his wife's intuition, but his son actually winning the French Open seemed way beyond the realm of possibility. Dad thought for a long moment. He decided that it would be too exciting to contemplate the conceivability of the victory, so he put the thought out of mind.

EUROPEAN VACATION

Mom and Dad traveled to Paris with me while my older brother, Carl, who was finishing his sophomore year at the University of California in Berkeley, stayed home. Carl, a standout player in his own right, had a tennis scholarship and was playing No. 3 for the Bears as the season was ending. José Higueras, whom we had hired to coach me throughout the clay court season, joined my parents and me in Paris. He would prove to be an invaluable resource.

Upon my arrival in Paris, I noticed that the French were feeling especially festive. The year 1989 marked the one-hundred-year anniversary of the completion of the Eiffel Tower. More important, the entire country was building toward the two-hundredth anniversary of Bastille Day on July 14—the bicentennial marking France's revolution.

All week long, my parents and I had been trying to snatch news about a *different* revolution fomenting elsewhere in the world—China. Since April, thousands of university students had been marching in Beijing and Shanghai, shouting, "Long live democracy!" More than fifty thousand students surged past police lines and filled Tiananmen Square in Beijing, embarking on a hunger strike and capturing the world's attention. For the past month, the student demonstrators had defied Premier Li Peng's order to leave or face military action.

Challenging martial law, hundreds of thousands of Chinese people remained in Tiananmen Square or blocked intersections to prevent troops from reaching it. A *papier mâché* "Goddess of Democracy," a replica of the Statue of Liberty, was erected in the square, and the world held its breath. The Chinese government called the statue an insult to the nation. Naturally, we were glued to CNN in our hotel rooms, watching events unfold in Beijing. My father was born in China before escaping to Taiwan in the late 1940s and later immigrating to the U.S. Mom was born in New Delhi, India, to Chinese parents. We were a Chinese-American family with relatives still living in China.

Meanwhile, I had drawn Eduardo Masso of Argentina as my first-round opponent. The French umpire introduced me as *Meek-hale Chong*, my last name rhyming with *gong*. That was fine with me; I was just happy to be playing in Paris. Eduardo won the first set in the tiebreaker, but I gained control of the match in the second set and didn't let go in gaining a 6–7, 6–3, 6–0, 6–3 victory.

After the match, Dad said, "Do you know who you play next?"

"No," I replied. "Did Pete win?"

"Yeah, and you're playing Pete."

I don't know how Pete Sampras felt about traveling seven thousand miles just to play the guy he had toiled with in the desert sun, but I figured that it had to feel pretty weird. I know it did for me, but I felt confident that I would win. At that time, I was already in the top 20, while Pete had just cracked the top 100. We had played probably twelve or fifteen times in the juniors (I won more often than he did), but this would be our first match as professionals.

Pete told the press that he didn't feel as if he was playing another pro. No, he was playing the archrival of his life. Great. We were long-standing foes living just thirty miles apart in Southern California, two young players touted as the future of American tennis, and only one of us could go on in the tournament.

Sensing something special between us, tournament director Patrice Clerc scheduled us for Court Central on a cool afternoon. I think the big stadium court, which seated nearly sixteen thousand people but was only three-quarters full, overwhelmed Pete. He made many uncharacteristic errors, and in a little over ninety minutes, I sent him home with a 6–1, 6–1, 6–1 whitewash. I would never beat Pete that badly again.

My third-round match, against Francisco Roig of Spain, was slated for Saturday morning, June 4. The sketchy news from Beijing was terrible: blood was being spilled as troops cleared Tiananmen Square. Hundreds were feared dead. The uprising had been squashed with military might.

A noticeable pall fell over the tournament, but the matches went on as scheduled. Everything clicked against Francisco in a straight-set victory. By virtue of winning my first three matches, I was pleased to have reached the round of 16. I had "played to my seed," which meant that as the fifteenth-seeded player in the men's draw, I had gone as far as I was expected to go. Waiting to devour me in the fourth round, however, was Ivan Lendl of Czechoslovakia, the world's No. 1 player. Ivan was a no-nonsense fellow who was all business on the court—and someone who rather enjoyed grinding his opponents into the dust of Roland Garros's gritty red clay.

I had one rest day—a Sunday—which was spent saying good-bye to Dad, who had to fly back to Los Angeles International Airport (LAX) and return to work on Monday morning. Dad didn't have much vacation time with Unocal, an oil company where he worked as a research polymer chemist. Although I understood, I wished Dad could be sitting next to Mom for the biggest match of my life.

A DATE WITH DESTINY

Ivan Lendl was the most-feared opponent on the tour. He cut you no slack and didn't suffer fools gladly. If you ran up for a short ball and hit a weak shot over the net, Ivan enjoyed ripping his forehand right at you from point-blank range. If you got smacked on the leg and received a little souvenir in the form of a raspberry-colored welt, it was your fault. You should have hit a stronger shot. In tennis, we call that "drilling" a guy. Well, Ivan drilled many players during his career, and if he happened to tattoo a Penn ball logo on your calf muscle, he would chuckle to himself.

Ivan had never drilled me in the two matches we played prior to the French Open. Maybe it was because I didn't venture much to the net in those days. Whenever I did cough up a short ball that left me highly vulnerable, he coolly knocked the ball past me for a clean winner. He didn't hit *at* me, and I appreciated that.

I think Ivan liked me, but perhaps that's because he didn't see me as a threat. Six months before the 1989 French Open, we had played an exhibition event in Des Moines, Iowa. Actually, I was a sub. Ivan was booked to play Boris Becker, who pulled out at the last minute. Would I play in his place?

Since I was sixteen and a newly minted pro, I had eagerly agreed to play. Exhibition or not, the match would be an excellent way to see how I sized up with the *weltmeister*. I played hard, but Ivan had way too much game for me, beating me 6–2, 6–3—a "routine" straight-set win in which I never really challenged him. Afterward, my mother and I traveled back to the hotel in a limo with Ivan.

We hashed over the match. "You know, with your game the way it is now, you have nothing that can really hurt me," he began. Ivan then proceeded to dissect my game like a CPA assessing a company's balance sheet: my forehand wasn't strong enough, my backhand landed too short, I had no net game, and my serve was a cream puff. "Plus, I'm able to control the points, so there really isn't any way you can hurt me," he opined. There was no boasting or bravado in Ivan's voice; he was just dispassionately assessing the state of my game at Sweet Sixteen.

I wasn't mad at Ivan. He meant no ill will or rancor. To a certain degree, I took his comments positively. Ivan stood atop the tennis world and had reached that lofty perch by hard work and a cold, calculating eye.

We played another match between that Iowa exhibition and the French Open, but it was part of an exhibition tournament in Atlanta, held on a green clay surface known as Har-Tru. This time I played really well, and I think I surprised him a bit by winning the match 7–5 in the third set. Even though that match wasn't for keeps, it still counted for something in my mind.

Now Ivan was waiting for me in the round of 16, a player on top of his game. He had won his first Australian Open in January, and in seven tournaments leading up to the 1989 French Open, had reached the final six times and won five. He looked determined and unbeatable.

Since we had a day off prior to the match, the break allowed the media to build up this feature match of day eight. "Lendl's not going to mess around with me," I said at a press conference before the match. "You can see it in his face. He has that look. He's not going to give me anything." Players of his caliber don't like to lose two times in a row to anybody, even if the previous loss was a non-tour match in Atlanta.

A few writers noted that our match had all the trappings of a "David versus Goliath" matchup, and I liked that allusion to the Old Testament story about a young shepherd boy taking on the world's most powerful and strongest man. Of course, it would take more than one shot to slay Ivan Lendl, so I girded myself for "a long, tough day at the office," as ESPN announcer Fred Stolle would say.

SHOUTS OF ALLEZ!

We were scheduled for the second match of the day on Court Central, Roland Garros's famed stadium court, where the Four Musketeers—Rene Lacoste, Jean Borotra, Henri Cochet, and Jacques Brugnon—had delivered France into tennis glory back in the late 1920s and early 1930s. Court Central seated 15,995 in those days (Roland Garros's stadium court was remodeled in 1998 and today holds one thousand fewer seats). The French fans are knowledgeable about tennis. If they don't like you, they rain whistles (their form of booing) and derisive jeers onto the court. If they like you, they can sweep you—almost *will* you—to victory with their sustained applause and shouts of *Allez!* The French sporting public had never warmed to Ivan, however, even though he showed great heart in coming back from a two-set deficit to defeat John McEnroe for his first Grand Slam title in 1984.

Since then, Ivan had added two more French Open victories, three U.S. Open titles, and an Australian championship to his résumé for a total of seven Grand Slams. At the ripe age of twenty-nine, Ivan was the most-feared player on the tour and the least appreciated by the fans. Perhaps that's because Ivan never played to the crowd, who, at Roland Garros, wore fashionable dark suits, splashy ties and scarves, and the latest designs from Paris boutiques. Ivan brought a businesslike demeanor to the court and allowed no person or distraction to penetrate his concentration.

On the morning of the match, I awakened to wafts of homemade chicken noodle soup cooking in our hotel room. Mom and I were sharing a single room at the Sofitel Hotel just off the Pont de Sevres, about a fifteen-minute drive to Roland Garros. Ever since I began playing out-of-town tournaments when I was eight or nine years old, Mom and I always shared a room to trim expenses. When I turned professional at age fifteen and began traveling for a living, Mom accompanied me to every tournament, and we continued to share a hotel room with two double beds.

During our two-week stay at the Sofitel, Mom, just as she had done every day during the French Open, had gone out shopping at a neighborhood grocery store, where she purchased a whole fryer and the necessary vegetables and ingredients to make homemade chicken noodle soup. Mom was absolutely ingenious in accomplishing this. Since our hotel room did not have a kitchenette or even a hot plate, Mom brought a rice cooker with her from California, which she could adapt to accept 220 volts, the standard electrical outlet in Europe.

After buying the chicken, she cleaned and prepared it, and boiled the whole chicken in the rice cooker. She then poured the soup base into a bowl and cooked the noodles separately in the same rice cooker, then put all the ingredients together to produce the best chicken noodle soup in the whole wide world. It took Mom probably ninety minutes to prepare the homemade chicken noodle soup—a tangible expression of her love.

"Here, you have to grow," said Mom as she handed me the whole rice cooker bowl. I could eat a lot, although I was only five feet, eight inches tall and weighed 135 pounds, meaning that I was giving away several inches and twenty to forty pounds to my bigger, stronger adversaries. While I sipped my soup and chewed my chicken, I noticed that Mom was very calm that morning. She always had an air of serenity about her before I played; today was no different.

At 10 A.M., I warmed up side by side with Ivan on Court Central. I hit forehands and backhands to José, took a few volleys, and loosened up my serve. We probably hit for a half hour before retiring to the locker room, where I showered and changed into new clothes.

As I put on my Reebok shirt with the slashing red and blue stripes and my white shorts, I mentally reviewed the advice my father had given me just before he left. "Offensive counterpunch," he said. "Take his speed and send it right back at him!"

"Right, Baba." I always called my father by his Chinese name for Dad—Baba. (My term of endearment for my mother was Mommy.)

"And go with your backhand down the line," continued Dad. "Remember how effective that was in Atlanta?"

Actually, I did. I recalled hitting several down-the-line backhands that caught Ivan flat-footed. "Remember, Lendl's most dangerous shot is when he stays about one foot to the left of the center of the base line," Dad continued, "because from there he can hit his forehand inside out to your backhand or go down the line into your forehand corner. Keep him honest. Move him around. Don't avoid his forehand, but if you hit to it, try to hit deep to his forehand while using your backhand down the line. If you can push him there, Lendl can hit his forehand hard, but he doesn't make you guess where he's going like when he stays near the middle."

I nodded. I knew when to listen to Dad's advice because it had worked for me since my earliest days of junior tennis. Throughout the years, Dad had videotaped matches, studied my opponents, and produced elaborate graphs and flow charts as only a research chemist could. "Last thing," he said. "Lendl does not go to the ball well on his slice backhand. He kind of pulls away and chips it back. If you hit the short angle to his backhand and he chips it back to your backhand, hit the hard two-hander down the line to put him away. Use that down-the-line shot against Lendl," Dad emphasized, "because it's your most effective shot against him."

I knew it would be futile to trade ground strokes with Ivan all day since he possessed more firepower off the ground. My strength resided in my ability to move the ball around, exploiting the angles Dad had described, and using my speed and mobility to set up points in my favor. I had to outthink and mentally outlast a physically superior player.

Nobody gave me any chance to beat him, which was understandable. The way I looked at my match with Ivan, I had nothing to lose. Though I walked onto Court Central in this frame of mind, I didn't want to go out there and simply "enjoy the moment" and keep a smiley face on while Ivan pummeled me. No, I wanted to win, and since I had beaten him in Atlanta, I felt there was no reason why I couldn't do it again.

The match started under gray skies, and we fought hard from the opening serve. The first two sets were seesaw battles, but on the big points—the deuces and the ad-ins and ad-outs—I never felt I could take the initiative. I competed with him up until crunch time at 3–3 or 4–4, but then he would turn up his game a notch and outplay me. Then again, that was why he was No. 1; he had that special gift to raise his game when he needed it most.

I lost the first two sets 6–4, 6–4, which frustrated me. The good news was that I was in the match and making him work. The bad news was that I would have to win three consecutive sets the hard way.

During the first changeover of set three, I made a short-term goal: *try winning a set*. That's all I wanted to do after losing two tough sets to the top-ranked player in the world. *Playing a fourth set against Ivan will be a great learning experience.*

It had always been easier for me to conquer mountains step-by-step. I learned this at a young age when I would come home from school with a ton of homework in my backpack. Discouragement was written all over my face when I stepped inside the front door.

"What's wrong?" Mom would ask in a sweet and tender way that only mothers can.

"Mommy, the teacher gave me so much homework again."

"Michael, you don't have to do it all at once. What's the most important thing you need to finish first? Let's work on that and then worry about doing your other classwork."

Mom patiently showed me how to organize my homework and figure out what was most necessary to do first—usually math. I would tackle my math homework for a while, and when it was done, Mt. Homework didn't look so overwhelming.

Now I was attempting to scale Mt. Lendl, but it looked as though I wasn't going to reach the summit before the match was over. I decided to keep plugging away and see what happened.

HOOTING AND HOLLERING

Late in the second set, ESPN began its live broadcast to the States—9 A.M. on the East Coast and 6 A.M. in Placentia, California, where Dad tuned in the match as excitedly as a youngster storms the family room on Christmas morning. He noticed that Court Central was packed to the rim, and that the French fans were into the match, cheering and whistling on each point, sometimes both.

I began playing better in the third set. In tennis terms, I began "imposing" myself on Ivan. My ground strokes had more depth. My serve had a little more sting. I began dictating the tenor of the points. Still, I could not get my nose out in front of Ivan. We fought hard to 3–3, with Ivan serving. In the first two sets, he came up with the goods on the important points, but this time I managed to induce him to hit a backhand into the net on break point. I was finally up a service break.

I consolidated the break, and then at 3–5, the points seemed endless as Ivan fought to stay in the third set. Maybe he sensed my game was building, but after three deuces, the third set was mine. More important, I would start serving the fourth set.

I glanced into the stands, where Mom was sitting next to José. It was just a quick glance; she nodded back, while the more demonstrative José yelled encouragement. I don't think Ivan was necessarily surprised to lose the third set because I had played much better, but that was the first set of the tournament he had lost. I'm sure he was ticked that I was still nipping at his heels.

Clay court tennis can be a fascinating chess game that tests shot making and stamina; now the battle was joined. Ivan ratcheted up the pressure. He had break points in the first, fifth, seventh, and ninth games of the set, but he either squandered them (his viewpoint) or I saved them by the skin of my teeth (my viewpoint). I sensed a bit of panic starting to set in. Ivan began questioning some calls and complaining about the playing conditions. "This court is absurd!" he screamed at one point, while taking a swipe at the dirt with his racket. Ivan was clearly rattled. He was letting little things start to bother him.

When you've played tennis for a while, you start to recognize what a player may be thinking or feeling, especially if you know his temperament. A turning point came at 4–2 in the fourth set, with me serving for the *fourth* time at deuce. Ivan whacked a backhand that he thought landed just inside the sideline, but the line judge ruled it out.

"Wait a minute," said Ivan, approaching the net with his arms outstretched. He pointed to the mark and asked the umpire, Richard Ings, to get out of the chair and take a look. Clay is the only surface that leaves an indelible mark on the court, and umpires often drop out of their chairs to personally inspect the mark and settle the question once and for all.

Don't ask me why, but the French tennis fans love to whistle derisively when a player disputes a call. Maybe it's because they don't want play interrupted or maybe they feel the honor of a French line judge is being questioned. Either way, they can let a player have it, and on this occasion, shrill whistles filled cavernous Court Central.

Ivan pressed his case. He implored Ings, an Australian in the chair, to overrule the line judge. Ings inspected the mark, then signaled "out" by pointing his right index finger away. This development prompted another round of French whistles while Ings bounded back up into his courtside perch.

"Ad-von-tahge Chang," said Ings, pronouncing *advantage* with a French inflection. A look of disgust came over Ivan, who continued to plead his case. "You cheat me every time! Every time, you cheat me!" screamed Ivan, clearly frustrated. Umpire Ings wasn't going to stand for that. Speaking in English, Ings announced, "Code violation, Lendl." Since this was Ivan's second code violation of the match, Ings further announced that I was being awarded a penalty point, the net effect giving me the game and a 5–2 lead. Ivan's eyes, set inside a prominent brow, looked ready to bulge out in anger. There was nothing he could do about it as we took our changeover break.

Suddenly, I was in a good position to win the fourth set. I tried not to think about *that* while I sipped a bottle of mineral water, which had a funny taste—very minerally. Still, I knew I needed fluids, especially if we had a fifth and deciding set coming up. First things first, though. I told myself I was up just one break, and Ivan was a dangerous player when he played from behind.

Lendl served to narrow my lead to 5–3, but I stayed the course and served out the fourth set. Court Central erupted, and ESPN made plans to stay with the match to its conclusion. By this time, Dad should have been driving to work, but he could not tear himself away from the human drama unfolding at Roland Garros.

The Deciding Set

As long as I live, I will never forget the fifth set I played against Ivan Lendl on June 6, 1989. To this day, people approach me and say they were at Roland Garros on that fateful afternoon. They shake my hand and then shake their heads in disbelief. If they are French, they often mutter *incroyable*. Unbelievable. That's how much the fifth set stayed in their memories.

Perhaps you witnessed that set on ESPN and can remember the enraptured fans leaping to their feet after yet another excruciating point between Ivan and me. Even if you didn't watch the match that day, you probably have seen two points replayed numerous times over the years. You know which points I'm talking about.

After winning the fourth set, it was my serve. Ivan and I went right back at each other's throats. Every point seemed like a war, with exchanges of ten to fifteen energetic shots the norm. We had played nearly four hours without a break, and we were battling fiercer than ever.

During that first game, shots of pain knifed through my thighs and calves. Cramps! I had felt some cramps at the end of the fourth set, but I ignored them for two reasons:

1. Mind over matter. To admit that I was cramping was to admit that I was losing my physical conditioning.

2. There was nothing I could do. Sure, I would gulp all the water I could on the changeovers, but I was on my own. Back in 1989, I could not call for a trainer and ask for a three-minute injury time-out.

If you have never experienced a major-league cramp, consider yourself fortunate. Cramps are like earthquakes—they come out of nowhere, shake you to your core, and leave you feeling absolutely helpless. Sometimes cramps are caused by tension, and this certainly was a tense time in the match. Either way, I had miraculously won sets three and four against Ivan Lendl, and all the momentum was riding with me. And now this.

On the 1–0 changeover I didn't sit down and rest, lest my legs stiffen up more and I go into full-body spasms. While I paced about my captain's chair, cramps were pulsating in both legs. The worst spots were in my calves and thighs.

I was losing mobility. This was not good because my game was built around my ability to scamper about the court, make incredible "gets," and dig balls out of the dirt. I unpeeled a banana and wolfed it down, then took a huge chug of water. I had begun eating bananas and French baguettes in set three, but I still felt as if there was no fuel in the furnace.

José had coached me on how to deal with cramps: stay calm, take deep breaths, and drink water. I closed my eyes and tried not to panic.

Lord, what do I do? I need Your help.

"Time," announced Richard Ings from the chair. I carried my towel to the south side of Court Central and tossed it to the ball boy. The crowd murmured because I was walking like Charlie Chaplin—stiff-legged and in obvious pain. Ivan, getting ready to serve, looked up and wondered what all the commotion was about.

I'm sure he noticed that I was hobbling about the baseline while I moved into position to return serve. I spun my Prince Graphite 110 Oversize racket in my hand while Ivan commenced his serving ritual. For probably the two-hundredth time that afternoon, he stepped up to the baseline, which he swept with his left foot. Then he reached into his right pocket and took a pinchful of sawdust, which he applied and rubbed onto his racket grip. Next he rotated two balls in his left hand against his stomach before depositing one into his left pocket. Finally, Ivan reached up and either rubbed his eyebrows or plucked an eyebrow—ouch! After going through these idiosyncrasies, Ivan was ready. I'm sure he developed that serving ritual as a way to set and ready himself mentally before each serving point.

A loss of mobility meant a change in tactics. Since I could barely move around the court, I began moonballing him—hitting slow-moving, rainbowlike balls deep into Ivan's court. I hadn't moonballed an opponent since the Boys 12s, but that was all I could do. The French crowd didn't like us lobbing soft balls back and forth. (Remember, if the French don't like something, they'll let you know by whistling their disapproval.) I tried to block them out because I was trying to win a match.

Interestingly, the tactical change flustered Ivan. He didn't respond well, and on break point, he flubbed a forehand into the net. He dropped his racket in disgust.

I was winning the battle, but I questioned if I would win the war. With each point, my legs tightened like a vise. My serve slowed *way* down, and Ivan broke back and then held to level the fifth set at 2–2. During the fifth game, my legs cramped so badly that I literally could not play. I looked for a way to stall for time. I had left my towel and a bottle of water with the ball boy in the back of the court. As my legs cramped in pain, I waddled over to the ball boy and signaled for the towel and water. I took a long swig and wiped off the perspiration around my face. I was taking much longer than the thirty-second limit between points, so Umpire Ings announced a time violation. At that point, I wasn't sure if I could play another point. I decided to give it a try. I took as much time as I could preparing myself to serve, praying that I would not have to *abandonné* the match, as they say in Paris. I knew that the calmer I remained, the better I would be since tension only made the cramps worse.

Ivan wasn't sure what to do. Should he change *his* game plan and throw in a few drop shots to make me run? Or should he keep moving me around the court and hope I would collapse, since I looked to be on the verge of doing that anyway?

Ivan chose to run me. Ivan hit a severe shot to my backhand side, but retrievable. After sliding into the shot, I felt a nasty cramp in my calf muscle as I plopped the ball back to the middle of the court. I yelped in pain and somehow kept my feet underneath me as I hobbled back to the center of the court while Ivan charged the short ball to his forehand wing. He must have heard my painful shout and looked up, because he jerked a relatively easy forehand wide, giving me an important game.

An Underhanded Ploy

We continued to battle in the fifth set. On and on we competed, each point a movie of the week, each game a miniseries. More often than not, we would trade high, looping forehands and backhands, and when I felt I could not make one more return, I would go for broke and try to hit a winner out of nowhere. When I did, the French crowd erupted in cheers.

I continued to shoot "arrow prayers" to God, asking Him for the strength to continue playing. I wasn't praying for victory; if the Lord wanted me to win, I would win. My prayers were for strength.

Somehow, I managed to build a small lead, 4–3 serving, up a break. Win my serve two more times, and I would defeat Ivan Lendl. Lose my serve and the score becomes 4–4; the momentum would shift in favor of the world's No. 1.

Ivan sensed that we had reached the critical point in the match, and I could tell he was bearing down. He had worked himself to 15–30. Ivan was thinking, *A couple of more points, it will be 4–all, with me serving. I win that game, and Chang's not going to be able to hold with that pressure against him, and the match will be mine.* In tennis, 15–30 is known as the "swing point." Win it, and it's 30–30, but in reality, the advantage returns to the server. Lose it, however, and you are down two huge break points.

What happened in the next ten seconds is something I will never be able to adequately explain.

I stepped up to the baseline, ready to play what was—up to that moment—the biggest point of the match. I set myself to serve, and then a lightning thought came out of nowhere: *Serve underhand!*

I never thought twice about it. I just did it. Instead of tossing the ball above my head, I dropped the ball toward my feet and sideswiped it just off my shoe tops, quick-wristing an underhand serve that fluttered at 40 mph over the net. Ivan, startled, still had the presence of mind to step up and give my weak offering a whack, but the spinning ball took a strange bounce and jammed his right hip. Instead of going for a winner, Ivan had to hit a controlled forehand up the line to my forehand. Since he was so forward in the court, he halfheartedly followed his approach to the net.

His ball was hit deep enough that I couldn't go for a passing shot, so I decided to dip the ball low over the net and force Ivan to dig out a low volley. The "book" on Ivan was that his volley was his weakest shot, so I thought I would take my chances on making him hit one.

I caught a break! My topspin forehand clipped the top of the net ever so slightly, causing the ball to fly a few inches higher than Ivan expected. He jerked his racket at the ball in an attempt at a backhand volley, but the ball glanced off the top of his racket like a foul ball.

Court Central exploded in its loudest roar, but I couldn't hear a thing because I was so excited. I shook both fists and exulted, fired up as I had never been fired up in my life. I paced and pumped my fists again, believing for the first time that the match would be mine. To say that Ivan was stunned would be putting it mildly. Steam was coming from his ears. He walked back to the deuce side of the court in a trance, and then pointed a finger to his head, as if to say, *This is becoming a mental battle. Stop letting it bother you!*

I had never *planned* to serve underhand. I had never hit an underhand serve in my life before that moment. I had seen it done in competition, however. Andre Agassi, when he was horsing around, had served underhand in junior tournaments in Southern California. Don't ask me why, but when I stepped to the service line at 15–30 against Ivan, the idea just popped into my mind.

With the passing of years, I realize how some may think that an underhand serve at a *crucial* juncture of the match comes off as audacious. It could have backfired and cost me the match: if the sidespin delivery had not jammed Ivan's body, he could have knocked it into a corner for a winner, and then *he* would have been the one exulting. I could see the French crowd turning on me—or worse, laughing.

My response is that it turned out to be the right serve at the right moment. History was made, and even after I'm gone and buried, the tape will roll that incredible point.

Incroyable.

A Giant Toppled

The score was still 4–3, 30–30, but my underhand serve destroyed Ivan mentally as much as the flat stone crushed Goliath's forehead. He fought on the next two points, but my momentum would not be denied. Now Ivan was behind, 3–5 serving.

He muttered invectives at the chair umpire and to the heavens. He glowered as only Ivan Lendl can glower. I worked him to 15–30 as we began a long exchange. I took Ivan wide off his backhand side, and he chipped his backhand cross-court. Remembering my dad's advice, I ripped my two-handed backhand up the line for a winner. Match point! I fought hard to keep the tears welling up in eyes from rolling down my cheeks. I was so close. I had also seen veteran players come back in this situation and win the match, so I knew things weren't over.

The restless crowd would not be settled. "Silence, s'il vous plaît," announced Richard Ings. "S'il vous plaît. Une petite silence. Les jouers sont prêtes."

Ivan missed his first serve. While he was taking his time to hit his second delivery, I moved in to receive serve. *Way in.* In fact, I took my place only three feet behind the service line.

I had moved way up in some of my junior matches, hoping to rattle my opponents or cause them to double-fault. The rules of tennis allow you to stand anywhere you want to return serve, but you are not allowed to try to distract your opponent by waving and making too much movement.

Ivan looked up at all the commotion. When he saw me standing right behind the service line, he knew what I was trying to do—distract him. He signaled to Richard Ings and pointed to me. Ings made no response. Ivan wondered if he should make a scene, but decided against that course of action, perhaps fearing the wrath of the French crowd. He shrugged his shoulders and reset himself to serve. He tossed the ball up and tried to hit a controlled serve anywhere in the box. Instead, his serve clipped the net and bounded two feet past the service line. Goliath had been slain! After four hours and thirty-nine minutes of battle, Ivan had cracked when he ricocheted his serve off the net cord and out of the service box.

My emotions completely took over. I fell to the clay in a flood of tears and lay on the court for several seconds before getting up and stumbling to the net to shake Ivan's hand. I cried tears of relief and happiness. Even to this day, whenever I really think about this match, the emotions simmer just below the surface. I was hurting during the match and crying out to the Lord to help me, and in His miraculous way, He did just that. I still don't know how I won that match, but then again, with God it's not so important to know why or how but just that He does.

Ivan was total class when he congratulated me at the net. It couldn't have been easy to lose to a seventeen-year-old at a Grand Slam event, but Ivan had always been extremely professional, and this time was no exception, especially after swallowing a bitter defeat. "He showed me a lot of courage and deserves credit," Ivan later told the assembled press in the interview room. "When you get cramps, it's very painful and it's almost impossible to play."

I walked off the court with tears streaming down my face as I acknowledged the crowd. I was thankful, yet exhausted.

After a shower and rubdown, I met the world press.

"Why did you win, Michael?" came the question from the rear.

"Because the Lord Jesus gave me the strength."

Total silence filled the room. The American writers in the room— Bud Collins with the *Boston Globe* and NBC, Thomas Bonk of the *Los Angeles Times,* and Nick Stout with the *New York Times*—had heard me talk about Christ and my faith since I had turned pro. But for the European tennis writers, this was over the top.

"What do you mean the Lord gave you the strength?" someone shouted out. I guess he wanted to be sure he had heard right.

"Just what I said. Jesus gave me strength to get through that match, and I give all praise to Him."

The next day, I learned that several French writers ridiculed me, and now my faith was center stage in Paris. French public opinion shifted against me. From then on, I would fight the French crowd as well as my opponent, all because I mentioned "Jesus Christ." I wasn't going to let it bother me or faze me since I knew the Lord had given me the victory in that match. I had to tell the truth regardless of whether people believed me—or supported me from the seats of Court Central. The noticeably cool detachment of the French fans after the Lendl match made me even more determined to win the French Open.

CHAPTER 2

THE ROAD TO A
GRAND SLAM TITLE

Defeating Ivan Lendl in dramatic fashion captured the imagination of the world's media. I don't know how many newspapers around the globe published a front-page Reuters photo of me falling to my knees moments after Ivan's double fault on match point, but it had to be a lot.

Now I was a marked man, and everyone wanted to talk to me. That night, as Mom and I were preparing for bed at the Sofitel, she heard a loud knock at our door. Mom answered in her pajamas, only to be greeted by a media mob complete with photoflashes and klieg lights. Mom quickly closed the door and called the front desk for help.

My agent at the time, Jeff Austin (brother of U.S. Open winner Tracy Austin), instructed the hotel to forward all media inquiries and telephone calls to his room. Jeff's phone started ringing around the clock. I could have done a hundred interviews on the day after I beat Lendl. I turned them down and did my best to cope.

While several influential French writers ridiculed me, the overwhelming majority of the press coverage makes me blush to this day, and many were respectful of my faith. Sportswriters dipped deeper into their bag of superlatives to find the right words to describe my titanic struggle with Ivan Lendl:

> Michael Chang said a prayer to make the cramps go away and then summoned all the courage of his seventeen years to defeat top-seeded Ivan Lendl today in a spellbinding match . . .
>
> —NICK WHITE of the *New York Times*

> His legs were cramping. He had tears in his eyes. The kid, Michael Chang, looked like he would rather die than lose.
>
> —KLAUS-PETER WITT of *Bild*, a Munich newspaper

> The small mosquito Chang stung the man who frightens children, Lendl. Chang was near death, but then he took his heart in both hands, said a prayer, and his prayer was answered.
>
> —*L'Equipe*, a French daily newspaper covering sports

> The youngest one ate bananas and poured water into himself while he crushed the biggest one. Afterward, Paris went totally bananas.
>
> —E. TRIER HANSEN of the *Politiken* newspaper in
> Copenhagen, Denmark

> Chang, leaking sweat and tears, gulped from liter bottles of water to keep his dehydrated body from turning into a salty pretzel of paralyzed muscles on a slow court the shade of Mercurochrome.

Despite cramps throughout the final set, Chang outlasted and outwitted Lendl, who ultimately cracked and choked, leaving viewers as well as participants gasping.

—BARRY LORGE, sports editor of the *San Diego Union*

If ever I needed a rest day, it was after the Lendl match. I slept in until nine o'clock and awakened again to the wonderful smell of Mom's homemade chicken soup simmering in her rice cooker.

I took the courtesy car to Roland Garros with José and Mom for a massage, and as I had done throughout the tournament on my day off, hit a few balls with José on an outside court. Once we saw the media horde gathering, however, we reversed tracks for the safety of the locker room, where we asked the tournament committee to organize a practice session at a nearby private club. We trained for twenty minutes a few kilometers away before the rains came and ended tennis for the day.

While watching a spring shower drench the courts, I killed some time with a French friend named Arnaud Deleval. I had met Arnaud, who was in his early twenties, a couple of years earlier at Chapman College (a small liberal arts university about ten miles from my home in Placentia) when I had dropped by the school's tennis courts looking for a game. Arnaud, a French native, was one of the foreign imports on the Chapman College men's tennis team. He played good tennis and was a friendly guy whose ego could handle losing to a high school kid.

Arnaud had witnessed the Lendl match, and he wanted to congratulate me in person. He also clutched several newspapers in the crook of his arm. After exchanging pleasantries, he said, "Michael, can I show you something?"

"Sure, Arnaud. What do you have?"

"A few of the French newspapers. You were front-page news today."

I had to admit that it was a bit surreal seeing myself taking up so much coverage—page after page of photos, stories, and commentaries. Arnaud pointed to several headlines and columns written about me. While I could make out a few words, my French wasn't good enough to comprehend what was written.

"Actually, Michael, some of what they write is not too nice," said Arnaud.

"Oh, really?" That surprised me.

"Here, let me read you an example."

Arnaud proceeded to translate a few sentences. I got ripped pretty good for my faith. Several respected French writers had a field day mocking my Christianity and my "childish" way of giving God the glory, but I reminded myself to pay them no heed. What they wrote didn't bother me, even when they resorted to racist stuff, like using the word *chinetoque* in a headline, which translated into the Asian slur "chink." I was called a "little slant eyes" with a "vicious Oriental mind." All this helped shape public opinion, but I wasn't going to change who I was or what I would say.

Our group returned to Roland Garros later that afternoon. I had heard people talk about the "fish bowl" effect, where your every move, every twitch, and every nose scratch are chronicled in breathless coverage. Moving about the grounds of Roland Garros, I felt like the largemouth bass and bluegill fish darting around in my aquarium back home in Southern California—I was swimming and everyone was watching. I found the entire experience rather astonishing: in just twenty-four hours, I had morphed from just another up-and-coming hopeful to this giant-killer swathed in Reebok clothes.

Like fish, the media need to be fed regularly, so I offered bite-size nuggets—a quick stand-up TV interview here, a mini press conference there. I noticed something interesting whenever I answered questions. If I talked about tennis, the writers scribbled away furiously, lest one of my words fall harmlessly to the ground. Whenever I mentioned the Lord, however, their pens and pencils stopped moving and the writers looked up to see what I would say next. They wanted nothing to do with my faith, but to me that was part of the story.

WAITING IN THE NEXT ROUND

Twenty-four hours after beating Ivan, it was time to start thinking about my next match. My win had propelled me into the quarterfinals, but this time around, my next opponent would be someone ranked *lower* than I, a player from Haiti named Ronald Agenor. ESPN tennis commentator Mary Carillo, always quick with a quip, called him the "Haitian Sensation."

Ronald, a bright-smiling twenty-three-year-old from Port-au-Prince, spoke five languages fluently and was a crafty player who loved the drop shot. He had reached the round of 16 at the French Open and U.S. Open the year before in 1988, so he was used to winning matches at Grand Slam events. His strength was an inside-out forehand that he loved to boom into your backhand corner, followed by a feathery drop shot that seemed to die just after it passed over the net. His Achilles' heel was his backhand, which he chipped without much pace.

French was Ronald's mother tongue, and he maintained a residence in Bordeaux. No doubt Ronald felt comfortable playing in Paris, and the French fans adopted him as one of their own. He was also one of three or four black players on the tour, and he and Yannick Noah of

France liked hanging out together and teasing each other unmercifully in the locker room.

The tournament committee put us out on Court Central, but instead of springtime skies we were greeted by cold and intermittent rain. Mom and José bundled up in heavy jackets while the match got under way. José was understandably worried that I would suffer a letdown following such a huge win two days earlier. One of the well-known secrets on the tour is that when a younger player registers a major upset, he cannot follow it up in the next round. It's too hard mentally to climb the mountain again. On top of that, it's one thing to win a big match against someone you're not expected to beat, but it's quite another to summon the will and physical energy against a lower-ranked opponent in the following round. The adrenaline just doesn't kick in as it does during the big upset. Learning how to follow up a good win with another victory or two is something that takes your game to the next level.

I'm sure Ronald knew all this, and two minutes after I shook Ivan's hand, he was probably plotting how to beat me. He viewed this match as a chance to make a major breakthrough into a Grand Slam semi. It had to be the biggest match of his life.

I started well against Ronald, but in the back of my mind, I was worrying about cramps again. My leg muscles felt tight, and I couldn't get loose in the cold, clammy conditions. I took the first set 6–4, but Ronald wasn't flustered at all. He began lengthening his ground strokes, driving me deep behind the court. Then he employed his deadly drop shot. Contrary to Ivan Lendl, Ronald wasn't afraid to use the dropper—and go to it often. I would spend a lot of time that afternoon sprinting toward the net.

When I wasn't making a dead run for his drop shot, however, I wasn't moving my feet nearly as energetically as I did against Ivan. Ronald took control of the match in the second set, winning 6–2, but more important, he was in total command. As we resumed play in the third set, he continued to move me about the court like a marionette.

It was starting to look like one of those days. We played through light rainfall, and with the balls picking up moisture, they became heavier and heavier on my racket. I continued to labor, and then I lost my serve to fall behind 1–3. Roland Garros's *terre battue* felt like red quicksand.

When the intermittent rain turned into a downpour, the umpire suspended play while I grabbed my racket bag and sprinted to the warmth of the locker room. Groundskeepers in overalls pulled a green tarpaulin over the court.

José was waiting for me in the men's locker room. I slumped on a bench and tried to collect my thoughts. José waited patiently for a few minutes. "You look a little tired on the court," he began.

"Things aren't going well."

"You're going to be okay, but you're letting the match slip away."

"I know."

"You can still turn this around. Just think about moving your feet again," said José, knowing that when I moved my feet, I got into position to hit *my* shots instead of letting the other player dictate the point.

I changed into a new tennis outfit and sought out Mom just outside the locker room. This was one of those moments when I really needed her.

We didn't say much because we didn't need to. When I mentioned that I was still worried about cramping, Mom said, "The Lord will take care of you. He always has."

"Thanks, Mommy." That seemed to take the pressure off.

It rained hard for twenty minutes. When the grounds were dry enough to resume play, we walked out to warm up again, but the rains returned, so Ronald and I trudged back to the locker room. It would turn out to be a forty-five-minute delay.

I felt much fresher when we resumed the match. Not only did the break come at a fortuitous time, but the rain delay allowed me to mentally regroup. Ronald won his serve to go up 4–1. *It's still only one service break*, I told myself at the changeover. Then I started to rally—really rally. I raised my game a couple of notches and swept the next five games in thirty minutes to take a two-sets-to-one lead.

The French crowd had been noticeably cool to me all day, not at all as excited as in the Lendl match. Then I gave them something to chatter about in the fourth set. At 4–4, 15–40, and two break points facing him, Ronald missed his first serve. Since this was a *huge* point, I decided to assume the Lendl Position, creeping up to within a yard of the service line. Ronald, clearly bothered by my boldness, steadied himself before making his ball toss, but just like Ivan, he double-faulted. The crowd whistled in disapproval against me—probably since Ronald was the underdog—but now I was serving for the match.

I won the first two points, but at 30–15, I missed my first serve. I was taking my time before offering a second delivery when I heard the Court Central audience make a loud commotion. I looked up to see Ronald, a mischievous grin plastered across his face, assuming the Lendl Position against me! He stood right behind the service line and challenged me to serve!

This development sent the stadium into a tizzy. This was a mental attack by Ronald, and I have to admit, a good one. The French crowd roared its approval, alternately chuckling and clapping at the incongruous situation. I waited for the noise to subside and decided I would *not* double-fault. I spun the second serve in, but I lost a long point and later the game.

The fourth set ended in a tiebreaker. I took an early lead, but he came back—courtesy of another drop shot. Then he worked himself to a 6–5 lead in the breaker, set point for him. I missed the first serve only to see him assume the Lendl Position again! I backed off the baseline and wiped my brow. I plopped in my second serve, but then he dumped the return into the net! The crowd thought, *Oh, I can't believe you missed that.* Neither could I.

Two points later, the fourth-set tiebreaker was mine, as well as the match, 6–4, 2–6, 6–4, 7–6. I breathed a sigh of relief—for winning and for getting through the match without cramping. I showered and then met with the media. This time, the questions centered around my "Lendl Position."

"I started moving up close to the service box in the juniors," I explained. "I would always play guys who were older than I. They would see this little squirt across the net move up, and they would get nervous because of my age and because of my position behind the service box."

"But isn't this a playground tactic?" asked a writer.

"I would never do that to insult or make fun of an opponent. But when you are desperate to win a point, you will do anything to bother the other player's concentration," I said. "A lot of times, they end up just plopping the serve in, which you can attack."

When the grilling was over, I decided to scout my next opponent. Court Central had a cordoned-off, players-only section high above the southern baseline, accessible from the locker room.

Playing below me were Mats Wilander, the defending champion who had won three of the four Grand Slams the year earlier, and Andrei

Chesnokov, a Russian player with an impish sense of humor. The players called him Chezy. As for Mats, he was the youngest French champion in history, winning Roland Garros in 1982 at seventeen years, nine months.

I watched both players play a dazzling, error-free set. The Russian seemed to have more firepower, however, and the way Chezy took his backhand on the rise and smacked it cross-court was a thing of beauty. *These guys look awfully good,* I thought as I returned to the locker room. I later learned that Chezy would brush aside Mats in straight sets.

THE RUSSIAN IS COMING

I expected a tough match against Andrei, and that's exactly what I got. We both had a lot at stake—a berth in the French Open final. The American writers were writing those "Can Chang become the first American in thirty-four years to win Paris?" stories, and Tony Trabert—at Roland Garros to commentate for Australian TV's Channel 9—was back in demand again. Everyone wanted to know whether he thought I had a chance because 494 Americans had failed to win Roland Garros since Tony's victory in 1955.

What I remember most about that match happened immediately *after* my four-set victory against Chezy, but I'll come to that in a minute. Chezy tested me in every way. His smooth, two-handed backhand gave me fits, and his forehand wasn't too shabby. He played tennis like a Russian hockey goalie—blocking and blunting my best efforts. I felt obliged to engage Chezy in a match of endurance, which boiled down to a critical series of points late in the third set after we split the first two. After three hours of slogging away in the hazy Paris sunshine, the unseeded Soviet found himself holding triple-set point against me at 4–5 in the third.

I felt as though I were being called to make a final stand. Not sure if I had enough stamina to win a fourth and fifth set, I took several risks during those three set points. Whenever Andrei hit a short ball, I pounced all over it. I claimed the third set in a close tiebreaker, but my run-down-everything style was sapping my dwindling energy reserves.

This match would have to be won in four sets, I decided. When Chezy worked his way to a 3–1 lead in the fourth set, I mounted a charge to catch him at 4–4. I reached match point twice a game later, but Andrei had an answer each time. I tried not to do anything rash and to keep my head, having come so close to claiming a berth in the finals. When I reached match point again at 5–6, 15–40 against his serve, I coaxed Chezy into netting a backhand, giving me a 6–1, 5–7, 7–6, 7–5 victory. Length of the match: four hours and nine minutes. I had a reservation to play for the French Open championship!

Mom rushed from Court Central to find a phone. She and Dad had agreed after the Lendl match that if I somehow clawed my way to the finals, he and my brother, Carl, would rush to LAX and take the next flight to Paris. Dad, who had been playing hooky from work that morning to watch the match on ESPN, told Mom that his bags were packed.

"I have more good news," said Mom.

"What's that?" asked Dad.

"You remember David Markin?" asked Mom, referring to the president of the U.S. Tennis Association (USTA). David Markin had taken a personal interest in our family, and he had been very good to us since my days in the junior ranks.

"Yes, what about him?" said Dad.

"David told me that he called Air France and reserved two seats on the nonstop this afternoon from LAX to Paris. I think the flight departs at four o'clock. He also said not to worry about paying for the tickets."

I'm not sure if Dad dropped the phone. A last-second ticket to Paris must have cost three or four times more than the normal advance-purchase fare—probably fifteen hundred or two thousand dollars a seat back then.

"You're joking," Dad responded.

"No, I'm not."

"I don't know what to say."

There was just one little hiccup: in 1989, France was demanding that all visitors obtain a visa from a French consulate before entering the country.

What a hassle. The only good news was that it was still early on the West Coast—not even ten o'clock on a Friday morning.

"Are you going to be able to get your visa in time?"

"I don't know," said Dad. "We will try as hard as we can. From my understanding, we have to go into downtown L.A., somewhere on Wilshire Boulevard, to the French consulate. We don't have an appointment or anything."

"The Lord will be with you," said Mom as she hung up.

Meanwhile, I felt relief more than anything. Chezy hadn't given me anything; I had to earn every inch of conquered territory. As soon as I walked off the court, I was quickly escorted to a TV studio underneath the Court Central bleachers for a series of quick-hitting interviews. Everyone wanted their three minutes: ESPN, NBC, France's A2 and FR3, Germany's SAT 1, the BBC, Sky Sports—you name it.

The studio was cool because those interviewing me—all wearing heavy television makeup—didn't want to sweat under the hot lights.

The set contained two oversize chairs: one for me, and one for my interviewer. "Is it always this cold?" I asked one of the technicians. After my fourth or fifth interview, my leg muscles went into shock. I attempted to stand up, but both legs cramped completely solid! I squatted down to the floor to relieve the pressure in my legs. When I tried to stand back up, however, my legs cramped solidly again. I was in *bad* shape.

Someone yelled for a trainer, and within a minute, Bill Norris and Todd Snyder, the ATP trainers, were at my side. They immediately knew my problem. They urged me—when I was ready—to get out of my squat. I waited for a few minutes to pass before attempting this difficult command. When I tried to stand up, my body went into complete body cramps.

"Michael, you're going to need to drink and walk," said Todd. "We've been here before." Todd had helped me get over cramps at other tournaments, but they hadn't been anything like this.

"I can't right now, Todd. I just can't."

I squatted again to take the pressure off the body cramps. When I attempted to stand up again, another wave of terrible cramps riddled my legs because my overtaxed body refused to send much-needed blood to my lower extremities. Those cramps hurt!

"What do I do now?" I asked.

"Keep squatting. We're going to take you back to the locker room," said Bill.

"How are we going to do that?" I couldn't walk, let alone stand up.

"We're going to carry you."

Each trainer grabbed me under my armpits, and as I remained in a midair squatting position, they carried my dead weight like a sack of potatoes out of the TV studio and into the trainer's room. Once there, I continued to hunch close to the floor as I gulped from a liter bottle of water.

"That's it, keep drinking your fluids, Chief," said Todd, who was always calling somebody Chief.

"When you feel up to it, try to stand up and walk," he added. "You have to start walking so the blood can get through. And drink all that you can."

The drinking I could understand. Walking would be a chore. (It is amazing how the treatment for cramps has changed over the years. These days, the trainers have IVs ready to insert into your arm, and an IV bag of fluids can rehydrate you in a half hour. Those IVs aren't for me, however. I *hate* needles.)

After an appropriate wait, I attempted to stand up out of my crouch. Several muscle groups balled up into knots, and we were all amazed at how grotesquely defined my quads and hamstrings were. I took a few itsy, bitsy steps, walking straight-legged as if my knees were locked.

"Good," said Todd. "Now drink and walk. Drink and walk. That's what you have to do."

I continued to chug-a-lug anything they gave me over the next two hours—Contrex mineral water, Gatorade, or any other sport drinks in the locker room refrigerator. Cramps rippled my legs and felt as though someone were trying to pull my muscle away from the bone. These cramps were way beyond anything I had experienced against Lendl. I grimaced and gulped more Gatorade, waiting for my body to absorb the liquids and for the cramps to abate.

"We're going to give you an ice massage," announced Todd.

"What's that?"

"Once the cramps subside, we're going to rub you down with ice. It's the only way your muscles can recover."

Todd laid me down on the training table and took a large ice cube in his right hand, and then he started rubbing my viselike thighs.

Normally, massages feel good; this was discomforting, but not as bad when compared to the cramps.

"You will be sore when this is over," said Todd. "The ice makes the muscles go numb."

He got that right. Following the ice massage, the trainers urged me to walk again. Todd continued to encourage me to drink liquids, and I complied. All the liquid intake, however, presented an overload to my internal organs. Every ten minutes, I excused myself to go to the bathroom, which I seemed to do almost nonstop for two hours.

After three hours of ice massage, drinking liquids, and walking around the locker room like an expectant father, I was ready to meet the beat writers, who had been waiting patiently. Since they heard that I was having "some trouble" with cramping, they all wanted to know whether I would be all right for the Sunday final against Stefan Edberg, a serve-and-volley Swede who was taken to five sets by Boris Becker, the German star and second-ranked player in the world.

"I should be okay for Sunday," I said. There was no way I would not be on Court Central at the appointed time.

"What do you think about your opportunity to become the first American in more than three decades to win the French Open?" inquired a scribe.

"I don't think about those things," I replied. "But it's definitely been a dream to get this far. I'm just going to go out there Sunday and try my best."

THE VISA SEARCH

Back on Wilshire Boulevard, Dad and Carl were doing their best to track down two visas so they could get on the Air France flight later that afternoon. They took their place at the end of a long line that snaked back and forth inside the French consulate's large foyer.

Within a few minutes, Dad received a tap on the shoulder.

"Excuse me," said a man in a navy suit who spoke with an obvious French accent. "Are you Mr. Chang?"

"Yes, I am," replied Dad.

"If you will follow me, please."

Dad and Carl were led to a side door and an office, where another consulate official was waiting to process their visa applications. Since it doesn't seem possible that someone would recognize my father, all we can figure is that someone tipped off the French consulate that my father and brother were coming.

Clutching valid visas, Dad and Carl rushed to LAX, where they made their Air France nonstop flight, and it was bon voyage.

The Final Preparation

I had a rest day before my Sunday final, but José wanted me to hit some balls to stay sharp. We didn't even try to play at Roland Garros. Instead, we were driven to the same private club where we could practice in peace.

I remember that Mom brought us lunch—something she had cooked up in her rice cooker back at the hotel. She mixed some Chinese chicken and a noodle dish into the pot, and the delicious meal hit the spot for me.

Dad and Carl still hadn't arrived at Charles de Gaulle Aeroport, so Mom filled me in on her morning. It all started when I woke up and mentioned something about getting a haircut before the finals. The bangs on my crew cut were starting to get a little long, and I didn't want to be bothered by strands of hair dropping into my eyes. Plus, I wanted to look sharp for such a historic occasion.

One of the unexpected amenities at Roland Garros was *coiffeurs* who cut the players' hair free of charge. While I practiced with José, Mom dropped by the salon to make an afternoon appointment for me.

The two women in the salon recognized Mom, but when they heard I wanted a haircut, they wanted no part of that.

"Michael can't get a haircut," insisted one of the hairdressers.

"Why not?" My mother was a bit perplexed. After all, we were talking about a simple trim.

"Because he's doing so well. Why change things? Besides, it would be bad luck."

"Bad luck?"

"Yes, it's bad luck to cut your hair before a match. You tell Michael not to get his hair cut."

This was a new one to Mom, who shrugged her shoulders and left.

Okay, so I wasn't going to get a haircut. It could wait a couple of days.

After lunch, we returned to the hotel to await the arrival of Dad and Carl and to watch the women's final. Interestingly, another seventeen-year-old player had unexpectantly come out of nowhere to reach the French Open final round—a Spanish retriever named Arantxa Sanchez. (She didn't add the Vicario to her last name until after the French Open.) They called her the "Barcelona Bumblebee" for the way she bounced around the court and played like a backboard.

Just like me, Arantxa was the surprise of the tournament, only on the women's side. Waiting to play her, however, was the female version of Ivan Lendl—a no-nonsense German named Steffi Graf. Few tennis observers gave Arantxa much hope beating the world's No. 1: in the twenty-two months leading up to the French, Steffi had lost just twenty-two sets. Arantxa had never beaten Steffi in three lifetime meetings. Winning two sets against "Fräulein Forehand," as Bud Collins had nicknamed her, appeared impossible.

There were two things I liked about Arantxa. No, make that three things: she played an offensive counterpunching game like me; she went into her final-round match as an underdog; and she was a Reebok player. I noted that she even wore a red-and-blue–striped Reebok shirt similar to the one I had been wearing during the tournament. I sat transfixed in my hotel room with Mom while Arantxa played her heart out for three draining hours before winning an enthralling encounter, 7–6, 3–6, 7–5.

After the match, she surprised me when she said that *I* had inspired her to victory. "I see Michael beat Lendl and ask, Why not I am beating number one?" she said in cute, fractured English. Arantxa had it all wrong, though: her match inspired *me*. I thought, *If she can do it, maybe tomorrow is my day.*

Dad and Carl had arrived at the Sofitel during the Sanchez-Graf match. It felt great to be together again, and I was really happy that Carl, who had just finished his spring semester at Cal Berkeley, could join us for this once-in-a-lifetime experience. When we discussed who was going to sleep with whom, Dad and Carl said they wanted to share a room and leave Mom and me together. None of us felt that it would bring bad luck to have Carl sleep with me, but Mom and I had gotten into a routine, and it didn't make sense to change things at this late date.

That evening about 10 P.M., as Mom and I prepared to turn out the lights and go to sleep, I took out my *NIV Student Bible.* I was in the habit of ending each day with fifteen minutes of Bible reading. I liked to learn more about God and how much He loves us.

I found it easy to concentrate on God's Word; reading the Bible provided a peaceful respite from everything happening around me. I don't exactly recall what I read that night, but I often ended my private time with God by reading from Proverbs. King Solomon's great wisdom from three thousand years ago had great application to my life.

I ended my Bible reading with a time of prayer. I had several things on my list, but praying for victory the following day was not one of them. God doesn't work that way. All I knew was that God was in control, and I would rest in that comfort. I went through my normal prayer routine that evening: praying for my family, thanking the Lord for loving me, and praising Him for all the blessings He had bestowed on me. I also lifted up the Chinese people during this difficult time following the tragedy of Tiananmen Square.

When I turned out the light, I heard Mom say in the darkness, "Good night, Bebe. Sleep tight." She pronounced her term of endearment *Bee-Bee*.

"Good night, Mommy."

THE FINAL MATCH

I can't say I slept like a log, but I didn't toss and turn either. I know I got out of bed *very* excited about what the day would bring. Breakfast was another rice cooker filled with homemade chicken soup; we weren't going to break a winning routine there.

Dad and I talked about strategy before we left for Roland Garros, but our conversation was more of him reminding me what had worked against Stefan back in March at the Indian Wells tournament. I had beaten Stefan, ranked No. 3 in the world, pretty handily—6–2, 6–3—

in the Southern California desert. It was the first time I had defeated him in three meetings.

"Just play like you did in Indian Wells," said Dad. "To beat Edberg, you need to return well."

Both Dad and I knew this was easier said than done, but if my return game was on, I had a chance to win. Stefan didn't serve hard, choosing instead to take a little off his serve and kick it in with topspin deep into my backhand corner. While his kick serve moved through the air, he moved with catlike quickness. Stefan closed to the net faster than anyone in the game; he seemed to be a step quicker than any other player I had confronted before. To counteract his quickness, I had to return serve a split second earlier and have him volley from his ankles instead of waist-high. Matches were won and lost by such a small difference.

"Move in two or three feet inside the base line and take his serve early," said Dad. "That way you can get to Edberg, because his serve kicks too high." Dad was correct. If Stefan's serve bounced high above my shoulders, I could not generate enough force to drive the service return down to his feet. Trying to take Stefan's serve on the rise was risky business, however, since it meant that I would have less reaction time to get a look at his service delivery. My hands would have to be very good on Court Central, but since I had successfully "picked" his serve at Indian Wells, I was optimistic that I could do it again.

Looking back, it's funny to see how God worked in my life leading up to the 1989 French Open. Before playing Lendl, Chesnokov, and Edberg, I had beaten each player once in the previous six months leading up to Roland Garros. Those matches were classroom lessons for me, and each win gave me a certain amount of confidence that I could beat these great players again.

Not that I went into my match with Stefan thinking I was a total shoo-in. Instead, I was neutral—neither high nor low. I knew Stefan would be tough, but I had beaten him before. That meant I could do it again. I warmed up on Court Central with José a couple of hours before the match, then retreated to the locker room for my usual prematch routine. About an hour before we were set to start, a tournament official found me in the players' lounge and said, "We have a 3:02 walk-on."

This meant that the tournament wanted Stefan and me ready to walk onto the court precisely at 3:02 to accommodate the television networks. We had to have our racket bags ready to go and have finished our prematch visit to the men's room. The 3:02 time was set to accommodate NBC, which would be broadcasting the final live back to the States (except on the West Coast, which had a two-hour delay). Dick Enberg and Bud Collins had the call for NBC's "café and croissant" coverage.

At 3:02, I followed Stefan as we were led from the locker room, down a set of stairs, and into the bright midafternoon sunshine that bathed Roland Garros. The temperature was in the low eighties, and the winds were calm. Although I was in awe of the occasion, I did not feel overwhelmed stepping out onto Court Central. This would be my fifth match of the tournament on the show court and my fourth consecutive since doing battle with Ivan Lendl six days earlier. The novelty of playing on such a large canvas was starting to wear off, which helped me maintain my composure.

During the five-minute warm-up, Stefan and I exchanged ground strokes, a few volleys, a couple of overheads, and a dozen serves. In the background, I could hear Stefan and myself being formally introduced to the crowd—in French—while we loosened up.

The French Open does introductions differently. Normally, the announcer says your hometown, your age, what big tournaments you've won, and that's about it. Short and sweet. At the French, however, the announcer recounts a round-by-round description of the tournament, which sounds tedious to me but had become a tradition at Roland Garros.

"In the first round, Chang defeated Eduardo Masso of Argentina, 6–7, 6–3, 6–0, 6–3," said the announcer as he began his roll call. "In the second round, he defeated Pete Sampras, 6–1, 6–1, 6–1." When the announcer came to the fourth round— ". . . and he defeated Ivan Lendl, 4–6, 4–6, 6–3 . . ."—Court Central filled with whistles.

Why are they booing me? I thought. *The match hasn't even started yet!* And it just wasn't an isolated whistle or a catcall from the upper deck. The capacity crowd filling Court Central let me have it.

Then I remembered: *l'affaire Lendl* was the match after which the French first learned about my faith. My interpretation of their shrill whistles—which were not universal, I must add—was that they didn't appreciate me being so bold about witnessing for Christ. I did my best to ignore their incessant whistling while I warmed up.

I must admit that it felt like the eyes of the world were burning a hole in my back, but I used that feeling to play inspired tennis against Stefan. After Bruno Rebeuh, a French umpire, bade us to *jouez*—play—I started the match with an ace up the "T," or middle of the court. Then I began smoking service returns all over the place. Before Stefan could look up, I snatched the first set, 6–1.

Things were going my way—including several net cords in my favor. After my fourth "lucky" net cord in the second set, the French fans began whistling. I exaggerated a shrug of my shoulders and outstretched my arms as if to say, "Hey, it's not my fault." Midway through the second set, I glanced at Dad and Mom in the players' box behind the baseline, to my left as I sat in my chair. José sat between my parents. I also noticed Carl sitting in the row in front of them. I didn't meet their gaze, however, because I wanted to remain focused. Their encouragement bolstered my belief that I could actually win this championship.

Although I felt I was on my way, Stefan shrugged off the one-sided opening set by serving and volleying with greater precision. He cleaned up his game considerably in the next two sets. I remember one point when I hit a forehand passing shot up the line. Stefan lunged for a backhand volley and popped up the ball into my midcourt. While I lined up a fairly easy forehand cross-court pass, Stefan swirled 360 degrees and intercepted my shot, knifing the volley for a winner. The crowd erupted in Stefan's favor. I shrugged my shoulders and told myself that Stefan was moving well.

Stefan pocketed sets two and three in convincing fashion. Agenor and Chesnokov had failed to win the pivotal third set against me after we split, but not Stefan. His aggressive, all-court game on clay was working with Swedish precision, and now I was in a hole. I felt that Stefan was playing great, but I believed there was still some tennis left to play. I would have to win two more sets the hard way.

Stefan made life very difficult for me early in the fourth set as he increased the pressure with brilliant forays to the net. Stefan earned four break points at 1–1, but I held him off. I had to save *five* more break points at 3–3. Finally, a break point at 4–4 would have given him the chance to serve for the French Open championship. Each time, I escaped the trap set by Stefan. If he had converted on any of those break chances, I probably would have been holding the runner-up plate.

On one break point, Stefan drilled a forehand approach deep into my backhand corner that I barely reached with both hands on my racket. I stabbed at the ball and watched it sail down the line—a wounded duck of a shot that was something between a pass and a lob. Stefan didn't know whether to volley the above-shoulder ball or watch my backhand return float long. He decided, in a split second, not to play the ball. My shot somehow caught part of the painted line on the *terre battue*.

I saved another break opportunity when Stefan came in off a great approach shot that took me *way* off the court to my forehand side. He pulled me so far off the court that all I could do was slap at the ball like a jai alai player. I flung the ball down the line into a six-inch gap—the only place on the court that Stefan couldn't cover. My slashing shot found the sideline for an unbelievable winner.

When Stefan had that break point at 4–4 in the fourth, I felt that I was called to make a last stand. After Stefan chipped and charged, I ripped a backhand missile down the line that the Swede couldn't handle. I pumped my fists and fired myself up again.

I held to go up 5–4. Where saving a break point had put some wind into my sails, fatigue was starting to weigh down Stefan's ship. He double-faulted twice, and at 30–30, I hit two forcing service returns that he punched into the net, suddenly giving me the fourth set! In just five minutes, I had gone from nearly congratulating Stefan for playing a fine match to being one set away from the French championship. I saw an opening to the finish line, and I would not give up until I beat Stefan there.

FINAL, FINAL SET

Stefan surprised me by breaking my serve in the first game of the fifth set. I had made one of my occasional advances to the net only to get whiplash when Stefan produced a wicked topspin lob over my head.

I saw him raise both arms in triumph. He felt that he had finally broken me—physically and mentally.

I needed to reel in the break as quickly as I could to stop his momentum. At the end of another long game, I returned the favor and wristed a topspin lob over Stefan's head to get the break back. I breathed in a sigh of relief when I got back on serve at 1–1. The next game on my serve was another long, combative one in which Stefan had a pair of break chances. When I finally held serve after four deuces, he looked visibly tired.

We had been playing for over three-and-a-half hours, grinding away at each other. It is hard to serve-and-volley for five sets, and Stefan was still coming in behind his first serve. I broke him to go up 3–1, held, and then built a 5–2 lead. Just like that, I was just four points away, and Court Central buzzed with anticipation that I would become the youngest male winner of a Grand Slam title.

A weary-looking Stefan looked like a half-chopped tree in the Bois de Boulogne that was ready to fall. He played several tired points in the final game, which brought the score to 15–40, two match points. Suddenly I became *very* nervous. My mind began racing, and I was so excited that I could hardly breathe. People ask me what was going through my mind, and I can't honestly remember. I was wired on adrenaline.

I took my place in the deuce court while the umpire petitioned the crowd for silence. I jumped up and down in place, then I crouched and waited for Stefan to serve; it was all I could do to keep my hands from shaking. He hit a kick serve up the middle of the court that took a funny hop. I stayed with the bounce and pushed the ball back to the middle of the court. Stefan hit a safe forehand that took me off the court a little, but I was so nervous I muscled my forehand into the middle of the court, but this time much shallower. Stefan moved on the ball and wanted to hit the ball behind me, but he stiff-armed his forehand into the middle of the net, causing bedlam to break out.

I had won the French Open! My first reaction was to turn around to my family in the stands behind me as my knees bent and back arched. Then I pointed two fists at them, not triumphantly, but more in a "Can you believe this?" manner. I turned and hustled up to the net for the traditional postmatch handshake.

"Congratulations," said Stefan over the din of the sustained applause. "Well played." The final score: 6–1, 3–6, 4–6, 6–4, 6–2.

Stefan isn't a man of many words, but I understood that was not the place for small talk. We shook hands with Bruno Rebeuh, but waiting for me next to my chair was Nelson Monfort with France's A2, who for years had been thrusting a microphone at the winners at Roland Garros. People were still clapping and cheering loudly when he predictably asked me how I felt to become the youngest winner of a Grand Slam. I said that I didn't think I could come back in the fourth set and that I didn't know what kept me going, although I *really* knew what kept me going.

Nelson Monfort simultaneously translated my comments into French, and a minute later, I slumped into my chair and swigged from my liter of water while I smiled at my parents. The French quickly prepared for the presentation ceremonies. In those days, the players walked up a stairwell to a special box behind the baseline where Philippe Chatrier sat, president of the International Tennis Federation; Juan Antonio Samaranch, president of the International Olympic Committee; various French tennis officials; legendary players; and assorted French celebrities—what the players call the "Monte Carlo set."

Princess Caroline clapped while I made my way to receive my trophy. Jean Borotra, ninety years old, and Rene Lacoste, eighty-five—two of the Four Musketeers for whom Roland Garros was built sixty-one years earlier—presented me with a large silver bowl mounted on a marble stand. I immediately raised the chalice above my head to the cheers of the crowd. Then I was handed an open microphone.

I reached in my pocket for a piece of paper. The crowd tittered, as if I was a schoolboy caught taking study notes out of my pocket during a big test. "This paper isn't a victory speech," I began with a sheepish grin. "It's just a guideline to what I'm going to say because after matches like this, you can't remember what you want to say."

Then I turned serious, and my voice quavered a bit. "These two weeks, regardless of what happened today, are really going to stay with me throughout my whole life. I would like to thank everybody for making it so enjoyable. I would like to thank my family and friends over here," I said, motioning to my right at Mom, Dad, Carl, and José.

I didn't think twice about what I would say next, although I figured it would incur the wrath of Court Central. "I also want to thank the Lord Jesus Christ, because without Him, I am nothing."

That statement struck a nerve! The cheers turned to boos and whistles, and while I'm sure a few people clapped, I sure didn't hear them. As for my benediction, I finished by saying, "I am looking forward to coming here next year, and God bless everybody, especially those in China."

Looking back, one of the good things about being so young is that I didn't care what the French crowd thought. Their whistles failed to bother me much. Maybe that was the Lord's protection during those early evening hours, but that's the way I felt.

The whistles died down as I posed for photographs holding my *coupe*. It seemed as if five hundred lenses were pointed at me, and photographers asked me to look their way, kiss the trophy, or hold it aloft. When I thought I was done, I began walking toward the locker room as I clutched the winner's trophy.

"Excuse me, Michael, but you don't get to keep that one," interrupted a French tennis official.

"I don't?" That was the most surprising news I had heard all day.

"Yes, that one stays with us."

"How come?"

"Because the players get a replica. And here it is."

The tennis official held a much smaller version of winner's hardware in his hands. At first, I thought the miniature trophy, inscribed *Simple Messieurs 1989*, was a joke. While my new one looked exactly like the one I had held before sixteen thousand at Roland Garros and millions around the world looking in on TV, it had to be one-fifth the size. I started laughing.

"You're kidding me, right?"

"No, I'm afraid not."

I had always dreamed of holding a Grand Slam trophy high in the air and taking it home with me. I shrugged my shoulders and hid my disappointment. Of course, I received more than a prized trophy or a rise in the world rankings. The winner's check of $291,752 more than doubled my career earnings—and certainly looked like all the money in the world to my family and me.

Waiting to interview me for NBC was Bud Collins, who brought Tony Trabert with him. "Why did you win?" asked Bud.

"To tell you the truth, I don't know why," I replied as I held the smaller trophy. "I do know Someone is watching over me. The difference today was so slight."

I was a bit embarrassed when Tony congratulated me. "I salute you because you are the first American since I did it in 1955 to win this men's championship," said Tony. "I was pulling for you and predicted that you would win today's match."

After I showered, there was still the obligatory press conference. Several asked about the whistles at the presentation ceremony. "People, in a way, are getting sick of me talking about God, but if I want to tell the truth, it is Jesus Christ," I said. "I give Him the credit. That's just the way I am."

I left Roland Garros with my family at around 9 P.M., with plenty of light still left. Reservations had been made at an upscale hotel restaurant, and in our party were my agent, Jeff Austin, and an executive from a tennis manufacturer who had been after me for some time to switch to their racket.

I didn't feel much like talking business, so our evening was spent enjoying the moment. I turned in soon after we got back to the Sofitel, but I had been informed that the first day of the rest of my life was already busy. The *coiffeurs* at Roland Garros were ready to cut my hair. A photo shoot would follow later that morning. The plan was for me to hold the French Open trophy—the big one!—somewhere in the park-like setting of the Bois de Boulogne. Then I had a live interview with the *Today Show* at 1:15 P.M. (7:15 A.M. EST in New York). I was booked for several other sit-down sessions as well.

When I left Paris on Tuesday, a full-page advertisement appeared in such publications as *USA Today* and the *New York Times*. The simple ad for Reebok displayed two boxed photos equal in size. One was an action shot of Arantxa Sanchez taken from her final match; the other was an action shot of me from my final.

The stark advertisement contained only one sentence of copy:

At 17, some go to Paris to study history. Others go to make it.

I had made history, but I had no idea what my future would hold.

• DIANA, DR. GRAHAM, MYSELF, AND CARL •

CHAPTER 3

FAME AT MY DOORSTEP

I left Paris for London with a suitcase full of expectations and as the topic of conversation everywhere. The next big tournament on the horizon was Wimbledon, tennis's oldest and most coveted title. During this time, I learned how powerful TV images can be. I received a letter from a young girl imploring me not to eat bananas with "dirty fingers." She had watched me peel banana after banana in my match against Ivan Lendl, break off the fruit with my right hand, and chomp away. "Don't you know that your hands get dirty from playing on the clay?" she asked.

Meanwhile, the mainstream media cleaned up when it came to creating "Changmania." Remember: this was a time when the fortunes of U.S. tennis were down, and people were asking who the next Jimmy Connors or John McEnroe would be. My story line proved irresistible. *Middle-class son of Chinese immigrants, raised on the public courts of Southern California, is pitted against stronger, taller, and older opponents. Relying on guts and guile, the pint-sized pro—who should be a junior in high school—becomes the youngest male to win a Grand Slam.* Those who had been following tennis closely, however, knew that I had been making waves since 1987 when I won my first-round match at the U.S. Open at the age of fifteen—the youngest male ever to accomplish that feat as well. My unexpected win then caused an excited reporter to ask John McEnroe, at the time the top American player, what he thought of Michael Chang.

"Who's Michael Chang?" replied a puzzled McEnroe.

Now that I was flying above the radar and being celebrated as the next American tennis hero, John knew who I was. Perhaps he thought I deserved to be knocked down a peg or two. At any rate, this time when reporters rushed John to ask him whether I had a chance to win Wimbledon, he issued a challenge. If I ever captured a Wimbledon crown on its slick grass surface, John said he would "drop his pants" on Centre Court.

Funny, but not a clear sign of respect. Then again, John likes to make waves. I remember a few years ago when John, commenting on the USA Network regarding a U.S. Open match between Dutch players Richard Krajicek and Jan Siemerink, said he would "stand on his head" if Siemerink came back from 6–0 in the tiebreaker to save six set points. Well, Jan did erase six set points, and the next day John ignominiously attempted to stand on his head in the broadcast booth.

I never dwelled on the slights and little digs from John; that was John being John, I felt. Nor did I feel the need to respond in kind. I do know that I felt as though I never got any respect from John until the time I beat him for the first time, which happened three years later at the 1992 U.S. Open. John, who was thirty-three years of age compared to my twenty years, had a great run during the summer of 1992. He was ranked higher than me when I finally got him at Flushing Meadow, which meant I was okay in his book.

NO CHANGES AHEAD

Back in England following the 1989 French Open, everyone wanted an interview, a few words, or a picture. Fans followed me everywhere and staked out the players' hotel. My agent carried a fistful of phone messages with him. I wasn't used to receiving much attention, so the brave new world I inhabited following Roland Garros took some adjustment. I remember talking with Mom, and we agreed that we did not want our home life to change or the lifestyle we had created on the road (Mom cooking for me, tending to my laundry, and generally looking out for my best interests). We even joked that my one-hundred-dollar monthly allowance would remain the same.

On a serious note, I didn't want to change as a person. Mature? Yes. Become a better person? Yes. Not become conceited or full of myself? Double yes. Still, we both knew that our lives had changed forever because of the notoriety of me winning the French Open at such a young age. There was little we could do about that. A media stampede followed me to the practice courts, traipsed around the locker room, and lingered around the hotel lobby. Setting boundaries was tough. Mom would cut off interviews in midsentence, but then the writer would dismissively mention in his story that his "ten minutes were up." Then there was the *way* I answered questions. Although I did not speak in "valley talk" typical of my teen brethren, I *was* seventeen years old, which meant I routinely punctuated my sentences with words like "nope" and "you know" and "for sure." I also added the useless phrase "and stuff" to nearly any word combination, so that I wound up saying things such as "I like to fish and stuff" or "My mother cooks rice and stuff for me."

Writers didn't hesitate to ask me to speak as an adult on a variety of topics, including my thoughts on whether Wimbledon should plow up its grass courts, or if I viewed myself as the future of American tennis, or what I thought about being the greatest Chinese-American athlete since halfback Johnny Chung starred on the gridiron in 1941. (Don't feel bad. I'd never heard of him either.) Most of the writers were no problem, but I was on my guard with anyone from the British tabloids, home to the world's most aggressive scribes. They struck me as a bunch that never met a fact they liked when it stood in the way of a good story.

Despite the around-the-clock media attention, two things happened in London that were very special—and wouldn't have occurred if I hadn't won the French Open. The first was being asked by Princess Diana to participate in a tennis exhibition that benefited one of the charities she was involved in. To meet a real live princess seemed like a dream, and she was as nice and personable as she seemed to be on TV.

The other event was being driven over to a London hotel with Mom and Dad to meet with evangelist Billy Graham, his wife, Ruth, and his top aide, Maury Scobee. Dr. Graham was in London for one of his evangelistic crusades.

Whereas meeting Princess Di was exciting, being introduced and shaking hands with Dr. Graham filled me with awe. I remember having the sensation that this kindly giant of the Christian faith could look right into my heart and see any unconfessed sins residing there. Dr. Graham immediately put me at ease as we made small talk about tennis and how my French Open victory meant that I would now be in the spotlight. He encouraged me to grow in my walk with Christ and stay close to Him.

I treated each of Dr. Graham's words as if they had been inscribed on stone tablets at Mt. Sinai. Yet the most enjoyable part of the evening was hearing Mrs. Graham describe how she had been born and raised in China for the first seventeen years of her life. Her father, Dr. L. Nelson Bell, had been a medical missionary in Tsingkiangpu, located in the eastern Chinese province of Northern Kiangsu. She mentioned that her father had been chief of surgery at the largest Presbyterian mission hospital in the world, and that the family had lived in the hospital compound.

My parents were fascinated to hear Mrs. Graham recount life in the China of the 1920s and 1930s. She and her family endured unspeakable hardships, pestilence and plagues, and unstable political and military turmoil surrounding the Nationalist government, the Communists, and the Japanese invaders. When Mrs. Graham expressed how her love for the Chinese people and their culture had never left her, we felt a familial bond with her and her husband, especially after she told us that she cooked simple but authentic Chinese dishes once or twice a week!

There was one other person I met just before Wimbledon started. I ran into Ivan Lendl in the All England Club locker room, and his face immediately lit up.

"Congratulations for winning the French," he said genuinely. "I'm glad you won it."

I thanked Ivan and once again was impressed with his character. I thought after the French that he would harbor animosity toward me because every time I turned on a TV, I was serving underhand to the poor guy or moving up to the service box just before he double-faulted on match point. Instead, he heartily gave me a verbal pat on the back.

HOME SWEET HOME

It turns out that John McEnroe didn't have to moon the world from Centre Court following the 1989 Wimbledon, but I did win three rounds, including an interesting rematch with Ronald Agenor, whom I again defeated in four sets. After I fell to Tim Mayotte in the round of 16, I felt I had acquitted myself well on the slick grass, where serves and power are the keys to winning, but not necessarily my strengths.

Six weeks in Europe was a long time to be away from home, and Mom and I couldn't wait to get back to Placentia, the smallest of Orange County's cities, with just seven square miles and fifty thousand residents. Sleeping in my own bed and feasting on Mom's meals sounded heavenly, and it would be nice not to eat in restaurants and to see how my fish were doing in my aquarium at home.

It turned out that the good townspeople of Placentia were bursting with pride that one of their sons won in Paris. Dick Enberg, who called the match for NBC, had said a lot of things like, "This youngster from Placentia just won't quit." The mayor, Carol Downey, wanted to give me a key to the city following Placentia's annual Heritage Day parade in October, at which I would be the grand marshal. (Placentia also named a street after me, but I've never driven on it.)

Not long after we arrived from London, I came home after a workout to find a dozen film technicians tramping in and out of our home, busy stringing cable from the production truck to four cameras positioned on our living room carpet. A television magazine crew was on hand to ask me how I got so good and why I won in Paris. Then I noticed a black stretch limousine parked out front, waiting to whisk me to the NBC studios in Burbank for a guest appearance on the *Tonight Show* with Johnny Carson.

Now *that* was something I was looking forward to. Like millions of Americans, I had grown up laughing at Johnny's monologues and skits. I knew he was a big tennis fan because every year he brought in a guest host while he traveled to Wimbledon. When the men's tour came later in the summer for the annual Los Angeles Open, Mr. Carson always sat in the first row behind the baseline at the UCLA tennis center.

"My first guest tonight is an incredibly talented player who captured the hearts and won the respect of fans all around the world a month ago when he won the French Open," Johnny began. "We're going to show you some tape here," he said, as he and the network audience watched replays of—guess what?—me serving underhand and creeping up on Ivan Lendl.

After Johnny finished his introduction, I walked out on that famous set and took a seat in the stuffed chair next to Johnny's desk. We exchanged pleasantries and talked a bit about the French Open and the Lendl match. "It had to be hard for him," I said, referring to Ivan. "He was playing a seventeen-year-old, he was up two sets, and now he's playing a little kid with cramps."

I was glad to hear the studio audience laugh. Johnny didn't like to structure interviews, preferring to chitchat and probe and see what developed. At the end of the interview, however, he asked me a question that his researchers had obviously fed him.

"I found out you don't have a driver's license yet," he began. "And you went out on a date. Who drove?" asked Johnny with a playful smirk and a raising of that famous eyebrow.

Nobody knew better than me that not being able to drive at age seventeen in Southern California was like living without indoor plumbing. *Okay, I'll play along.* "Actually, on my last date, my parents drove us." The audience guffawed and again the famous eyebrow twitched after hearing that revelation, which, I have to admit, was pretty funny. Fortunately, our time was up, so I didn't have to embarrass myself entirely. I would have told Johnny that Mom and Dad drove me to her house, and then they dropped us off at a nearby mall, where we ate at a restaurant and took in a movie. Then I called them to pick us up.

It was no big deal, Mr. Carson. I promise.

A THANKSGIVING SERVICE

A day after appearing on the *Tonight Show*, Mom, Dad, Carl, and I drove ninety minutes north to Thousand Oaks, located at the western end of the San Fernando Valley. We pulled into the parking lot of the Chinese Christian Church of Thousand Oaks, where family and friends were waiting to greet us. A thanksgiving service was planned on this Saturday evening—a service to express our great appreciation to God for what happened at Roland Garros.

The Chinese Christian Church was cofounded by my grandfather Ke-Wu Chang in 1981. I never called him Grandfather, however. Instead I used a Chinese term of endearment—"Gohng-Gohng." My grandfather has a daughter, Aunt Rebecca, who lives with her family in Thousand Oaks as well, so I always enjoyed family visits when I was growing up. Aunt Rebecca has three children, and my first cousins are Jimmy, Joe, and Jerry. I've always been close to them.

Gohng-Gohng is the patriarch of the Chang family, and deservedly so. He is about the same age as Ruth Graham, grew up in the Guangdong province, and raised a family in Choutzou. During the mid-1940s, Gohng-Gohng's mother became very sick with cancer, which, in those days of primitive medicine, was tantamount to a death sentence.

My great-grandmother was a Buddhist, as were all her family and children. When she learned she had cancer, a caring Christian woman shared the good news of Jesus Christ with her, and my great-grandmother became a Christian. This development greatly surprised everyone in the family, but then they were shocked when my great-grandmother's cancer went into remission. The whole family converted from Buddhism to Christianity after witnessing this miracle.

Gohng-Gohng's family produced alcohol for industrial use and sugar cane for domestic consumption, and by Chinese standards were very wealthy. They, along with all the Chinese people, found themselves in a raging civil war between Mao Tse-tung's Communist forces and the Nationalists headed by Chiang Kai-shek. When Mao took the upper hand in the conflict, Gohng-Gohng and his family were caught in the crosshairs because they were landowners. Chiang Kai-shek and his supporters escaped to Taiwan in 1949, and my family wasn't far behind them. They had to leave everything behind—including all their money—when they fled to the island nation.

Dad was about seven years old when the family arrived in Taiwan. (One of his sisters was left behind and has since come to live in the States.) Born in Canton in 1942, he was the third in the line of six children. I don't know much about Dad's childhood, except that his family rebounded and prospered in Taiwan.

Meanwhile, another Chinese family sought safe harbor in Taiwan when Mao took over in the late 1940s. Michael Tung, a Chinese diplomat who once served as the ambassador to Santo Domingo in the Dominican Republic, resettled in Taipei with his family. Betty Tung, the second of four children, had been born in 1944 in New Dehli, India, while the family was in the midst of a wartime diplomatic trip.

My future mother and father did not know each other in Taiwan, but they both settled in the New York City area. Mom arrived in 1959 as a fifteen-year-old girl; Dad arrived eight years later in 1966 when he was twenty-four years old. They each arrived in a foreign land where they understood neither the language nor the Western culture. Mom's family received special consideration in being allowed to immigrate to the U.S., while Dad was allowed into the U.S. on a student visa. The Tung family moved to Forest Hills, New York, considered part of New York City, while my father attended graduate school at Stevens Institute of Technology in nearby Hoboken, New Jersey. Dad was earning an advanced degree in chemical engineering. Mom had a degree in medical technology from the University of Minnesota as well.

My father sings very well, and one weekend he met a young woman named May Tung at a social for Chinese-speaking families. They struck up a conversation, and at the end of the evening, May suggested that Joe Chang meet her sister Betty, who also loved music.

I'm not sure if a little matchmaking wasn't going on, but Joe and Betty agreed to the blind date. The young couple hit it off. It must have been love at first sight because they married within six months of meeting each other.

They moved into a small apartment, and until their first child, Carl, arrived two-and-a-half years later, Mom worked in an endocrinology lab while Dad labored at Reichhold Chemical by day and pursued his master's degree at Stevens by night. Dad always had something on the side to make ends meet. They were just another young, Asian immigrant couple struggling to make their way, but they were grateful to chase the American dream in freedom.

THE AWESOMENESS OF GOD

My parents, along with several hundred friends and family members, filled the Chinese Christian Church sanctuary in Thousand Oaks for what turned into a poignant, two-hour thanksgiving service that acknowledged and praised God for what had happened in Paris.

I sat in the front row with my family, trying to keep my emotions from rising quickly to the surface. The awesomeness of God filled my heart. That He would choose to bless me in such an incredible way didn't seem possible, nor did I deserve it. God had worked through me for His purpose, though I wasn't sure what that purpose was, given my age and immaturity. Meanwhile, I was grateful for the opportunity to praise God and give Him the glory.

Our family was asked to come to the pulpit and say a few words. Dad chose to speak in English, so a man provided a simultaneous translation into Mandarin. Mom chose to speak in her mother tongue, and the same fellow translated her comments into English.

When it was my turn to take the pulpit, I found it hard to look up and face the full congregation. One reason was that I was still painfully shy standing up in front of audiences; the other was that I had had very little experience with public speaking.

I decided to begin by not assuming anything. "If there are any of you who don't know me, my name is Michael Chang," I began. "I'm seventeen years old, and I'm a professional tennis player."

That was like telling this audience that the traffic on the Ventura Freeway always got heavier at five o'clock, but I pressed on. "I want to begin by thanking the Lord Jesus Christ because without Him, I am nothing." I meant every word.

I then asked a series of rhetorical questions. "Was it coincidence that I was able to beat Ivan Lendl even though I was cramping so severely I thought I might not be able to win another point?"

The audience politely shook their heads.

"Was it coincidence that I came from behind to beat Ronald Agenor, Andrei Chesnokov, and Stefan Edberg? Was it coincidence that I saved so many break points?"

"No," said the audience.

"Of course those weren't coincidences. That wasn't just me playing in Paris. Jesus Christ is alive and well!"

I was embarrassed by the thunderous applause, and when I finished, I felt humbled that I could take part.

The thanksgiving service was followed by a reception in the fellowship hall, where a banquet of Chinese food awaited. I filled two plates with great food and took a place at one of the large rectangular tables with my parents and relatives. If I could have read Gohng-Gohng's mind, I'm sure he was thinking about how far our family had traveled to reach this amazing point in history.

The Early Days

I was born on Tuesday, February 22, 1972, at St. Mary Hospital in Hoboken. My claim to fame was that I was born in the same town as Old Blue Eyes—Frank Sinatra. You could also say that deuces were wild when I was born:

- I was the second child and the second son.
- I was born at 2:00 in the afternoon on 2/22/72—February 22, 1972.

- I was 22 inches long and weighed 7 pounds (112 ounces), 12 ounces (or a total of 124 ounces).
- I was named after my grandfather Michael Tung, so in a way, I'm Michael II.
- There is one other "two" I have to mention about my life, but it's one that bugs me because I would have preferred a higher number: my highest world ranking has been No. 2.

When I joined the family, my older brother, Carl, was exactly three years and nine days older than I. When I was six months of age, an event happened that changed how Mom viewed the nest she was building for her young robins. Burglars entered our modest home in New Jersey and ransacked the drawers, looking for valuables. The good news was that no one was home when this happened. However, when Mom discovered the break-in, she was shocked to see dresser drawers tipped over and her family's prized belongings tossed everywhere. Mom never slept in our rental home again because she was too afraid to step into the vandalized house. We moved in with her parents just over the Hudson River in Bayside, New York, for six months.

I'm told that I was a pretty stubborn child, but in a positive way. My grandmother Dorothy Tung tells the story of caring for me when I was eight months old. It seems that my parents had put me on a feeding schedule, and my first bottle of the day arrived at 6 A.M. Not a minute before, and not a minute after. Let's just say I had gotten used to when that first bottle arrived.

When Daylight Savings Time occurred in April, I stirred in my crib at 6 A.M. and fussed for my feeding. I was sleeping in Grandma's room, so I woke her up. After all, I was hungry, but it was 5 A.M. for her. In her view, she was entitled to another hour of sleep.

"I'm sticking to the clock," she informed me, which meant I would have to wait an hour before my first bottle. I'm told that I received this news with equanimity. Instead of screeching to the high heavens for my bottle, I jammed my right thumb into my mouth and sucked on it for the next hour to hold me over.

I barely remember anything about my toddler years. I'm told that I liked Tonka trucks and teddy bears and agreed to eat my vegetables because I wanted to be like Popeye. During this time, my parents started to pick up the sport of tennis. Mom was actually the first person in our family to play. She bought an old wooden racket at a rummage sale for one dollar and began hitting against a wall at her old high school. Later on, when Dad gave the racket a try, he liked the feel of the solid whack of a racket against a tennis ball.

My parents didn't have much time to play tennis, however. They were up to their armpits with diapers and trying to keep up with two lively toddlers running around the house. Like many immigrant families, they were struggling to get on their feet financially and dreamed of one day getting a place of their own.

Dad began looking for a new job. He soon turned his sights on 3M, a huge conglomerate that produced everything from Scotch tape to the synthetic material used in the space boots worn by astronaut Neil Armstrong when he walked on the moon in 1969. The company, headquartered at the 3M Center in Saint Paul, Minnesota, stood at the threshold of new growth in the early 1970s. Dad sent in his résumé, and after a couple of interviews, was hired as a chemical engineer. We were on the move, but all Dad knew about Minnesota was that the

Gopher State's harsh winters made the Empire State's wintertime weather look like child's play.

FAMILY CHEMISTRY

The same year that we moved to Woodbury (a Saint Paul suburb) in 1974, Dad was swept up by the tennis boom. The game had gone "open" in the late 1960s when tournaments began allowing the world's best players (who were professionals) to compete head-to-head against amateur players (who were paid modest amounts under the table).

Suddenly, the public was fascinated to watch such Australian greats as Rod Laver and Ken Rosewall compete again at Wimbledon and the U.S. Open against up-and-coming stars such as Arthur Ashe and Stan Smith. Tennis tournaments began popping up all over TV. Dad, like millions of baby boomers in their twenties and thirties, was attracted to this "sport of a lifetime" that consisted of quick, almost savage-like action followed by relatively tranquil intervals. He found tennis to be a fiercely competitive game filled with great mental stimulation.

Dad, who had played tennis a few times in New Jersey, became addicted to the sport after we moved to Woodbury. Of course, the tennis season wasn't long in Minnesota's northern climes, but Dad played in company tournaments, set up singles matches, and spent his spare time reading books and magazines about his new favorite sport.

Since Dad was playing so much tennis on the weekends at the local parks, Mom suggested that he take us boys along as well. I imagine that it wasn't too long before Carl and I clamored, "Me, too, Baba! We want to play!"

I was in the first grade, six years old at the time, when I first swung a racket. Dad took a ball hopper and filled it with old tennis balls, and then drove us over to some public courts. I remember hitting the ball into the court right away. I think I didn't find tennis that hard because Dad had played Ping-Pong with me before I ever hit a tennis ball. He had set up a Ping-Pong table in the basement and then found a chair for me to stand on. Then we batted balls back and forth across the net.

Carl and I stood on the same side of the tennis court with Dad and hit forehands and backhands pitched our way. Carl liked to hit the ball harder, but my style, even back then, was to get a lot of balls back in play. When he saw how much fun we were having, Dad opened up his wallet and sprang for a few lessons. Just one problem: we couldn't afford for *both* of us to take lessons from a pro named Ernie at Phelan Tennis Club, so Dad and I did the next best thing. We sat quietly on the court and watched Carl be schooled on his forehand and backhand ground strokes for an hour. Dad took notes while I paid attention to what the pro was saying. Afterward, Dad tried to teach me what Carl had learned that day.

I was still playing with a wood racket in those days, but everyone was talking about the introduction of the Prince racket—the first frame with a large-size head and huge string bed. I wanted a Prince too.

"Baba, can't you get me a Prince?"

"I won't let you switch to a Prince until your head gets bigger than the head of the racket," Dad deadpanned.

How was my head going to grow larger than a Prince racket? Dad, of course, was kidding, but to a first grader, I really wondered if that was possible. When Dad saw my quizzical look, he said, "Michael, I'm just joking. We can look at getting a Prince racket for you."

Dad was always pulling my leg. One time I swallowed a grape seed, and Dad said, "Oh, I don't know if you should have done that, Michael. Be very careful because that seed could grow out of your head." Dad loved to tease me.

When fall arrived and ended outdoor tennis until Easter, I devised an indoor version in our basement using a sponge-like Nerf ball. Like most Minnesota homes, our house had a basement with plenty of room for me to bat a Nerf ball around. Every day I rushed home from school before Mom and Dad arrived home from work, grabbed my racket and yellow Nerf ball, and disappeared to the basement, where a new world came alive.

My imagination was especially vivid in those days. Each afternoon, I played "matches" against Jimmy Connors or Bjorn Borg. Since each match was played at Wimbledon or the U.S. Open, I played best of five sets. I "served" by starting a rally against the wall, and then I played my heart out, keeping score point by point. My imagination ruled. If the shot came right back to me and bounced on the floor, the ball was still in play—unless I imagined that my shot was a winner. If my shot hit the front wall and ricocheted to a side wall, that meant Borg had missed and his shot was out. I played complete matches in my mind. Sets that I won were always 7–6—usually seven points to five in the closest of tiebreakers. Sets that I lost were always a "love" set—6–0. I guess I wanted to get them over with quickly.

Most afternoons my matches involved an astonishing comeback that left the gasping fans standing on their feet, cheering each incredible exchange, imploring me to come back against all odds, and then hailing me in victory. I would always fall behind two-sets-to-love, but that was just setting the stage for another miraculous rally over five tortuous sets.

I can still picture our family basement in my mind's eye today. I played almost every day after school—except at night. I needed to see daylight coming through one of the windows; otherwise, I was too scared to go downstairs into the dark, dark pit. I really believed that some bogeyman lived down there.

Right from the start I hit my backhand with two hands, just like Bjorn did with his black-painted Donnay racket. I loved scampering around the basement, trying to keep the Nerf ball alive and making instantaneous decisions about whether I had won or lost the last point. I found that my basement games improved my hand-eye coordination because outside on a *real* tennis court, I was improving quickly. Within a year of being introduced to tennis, Carl and I were taking home wood-and-plastic junior tournament trophies nearly every weekend, and people were telling my parents that they had a couple of prodigies on their hands. Unfortunately, the Land of 10,000 Lakes turned out to be a small pond when it came to junior tennis.

Late one night, after Carl and I had gone to bed, Mom and Dad wondered what to do.

"What are our options?" my mother asked.

"We could move to California," Dad mused. "There the boys could play year-round, and the junior competition is the best in the world." As usual, Dad had done his homework.

"Can we afford it?"

"I don't know," said my father. "It will take some sacrifices on our part."

"*Mung mu san tien,*" said Mom, which was a Chinese saying that means a mother will move many times just for the sake of her children. Mom, who was committed to building a nest for her family, was willing to pull up stakes and move the family out west if it would give her sons a chance to blossom in more fertile tennis ground.

CALIFORNIA DREAMING

In the summer of 1979, we moved to La Costa, a sun-kissed suburb in San Diego's North County. We lived just a couple of miles east of the La Costa Resort, where Jimmy Connors had taken lessons from Pancho Segura, La Costa's venerable pro. Pancho, a bandy-legged Ecuadorian who hit with two hands off both wings, had spent his younger days barnstorming the country in the back of Jack Kramer's station wagon. That was the time when "professional tennis" was a series of one-night exhibitions in towns like Davenport, Iowa, and Bakersfield, California. Have racket, will travel.

My parents couldn't afford to join La Costa or have me take lessons from Pancho, but being in San Diego gave me access to players who were taking lessons from Pancho. The upgrade in competition was everything that our family hoped for, and soon our weekends were booked with tournaments from Chula Vista to North Hollywood. You could play a junior tournament nearly every weekend of the year in Southern California, if you wanted to.

We did join an inexpensive tennis club shortly after we moved to La Costa—the San Dieguito Tennis Club in Encinitas. Carl and I took some lessons from the club pro, Brad Humphreys, and we played sets against each other and other juniors after school. Dad organized our games, oversaw our lessons, kept an eye on our progress, and fed us balls during drill sessions. After a couple of years at the San Dieguito Tennis Club, we moved over to the Cardiff Courts Racquet Club, where I still mainly practiced with Carl.

Please don't get the idea that everything was tennis, tennis, tennis in the Chang household. School was very important since we weren't allowed to play tennis or go out with our friends unless we kept up our grades. Poor schoolwork also meant no time for the family hobby—fishing. You would also think that moving to within a few miles of the California coastline could have turned me into a beach rat, but that never happened. I think it's because I wasn't the world's greatest swimmer. My friends in school always teased me for swimming with my head out of the water—a glorified dog paddle. Mom enrolled me in swim lessons at the local YMCA, but that didn't help.

Our family liked going to La Jolla Shores beach, where consistent but gentle waves were perfect for boogie boarding or treading out into the ocean. Something in the sand or water, however, never agreed with me, and I would often become nauseous at the beach. Even when we just walked along the tide pools and tried to catch fiddler crabs, I got bad stomachaches from being around the Pacific Ocean.

My parents were probably just as glad that I didn't have aspirations of becoming a beach bum. I don't think they worried about it. We were a close-knit, Asian-American family that believed children should have dreams, and dreams should never be discouraged. I know that whenever I talked about playing the U.S. Open someday or going up against Jimmy Connors, my parents never brushed me off. They encouraged me to aim high and do my best—but not forget that it would take a lot of work to reach my goals.

My parents were loving but firm. Like all children, Carl and I had our moments testing them, and when we stepped over the line, we were disciplined. I can only remember a couple of occasions when I received a severe punishment. One time when I had disobeyed, my father announced that I would receive a Chinese form of punishment called *fa-gua*. Dad directed me to kneel on the floor and stretch my arms in front of me. "You will keep your arms out as long as I want," he announced. Boy, it seemed like a long time until Dad declared the *fa-gua* was over. Hopefully, I had learned my lesson.

The other occasion had happened when I was much younger in Minnesota. Whenever Carl and I got into trouble, we had to sit in the kitchen with the lights off. We didn't like that at all since it was right next to the basement. Mr. Bogeyman was down there when it was dark!

Carl and I learned to respect our parents and their rules from an early age, which set the tone for an orderly and loving home. We knew that Mom and Dad would always support us emotionally and physically. In the Asian culture, the children come first, and if a child enjoys doing a particular activity, then the parents will take the time and spend money to help him become good at it.

"If you are going to pick a career," said Dad, "we don't care what you want to be. But whatever you pick, we want you to try to be the best at it."

In second grade at Flora Vista Elementary School in nearby Encinitas, I received an assignment to write about my dreams. I wrote about playing at Wimbledon, and in the finals of this magical tournament, I stood across the net from John McEnroe, headband and all. Like my basement Grand Slam matches, I lost the first set 6–0, but then I won the next three 7–6, 7–6, 7–6. As I recall, he did not drop his pants after we shook hands.

MAKING ENDS MEET

As I became older, I began noticing what my parents did to make ends meet and keep Carl and me in Court Casual tennis shorts and new sneakers. Mom was a chemist and a medical technologist by training, but to work flexible hours, she took on several odd jobs.

For instance, several nights a week she was a hostess at a seafood restaurant in Oceanside. She taught cooking classes at a Chinese restaurant a couple of afternoons a week, where friends showed up to learn how to cook something as simple as fried rice to as complex a dish as orange beef. I can remember helping her set up for her cooking classes during my school vacation. I was in a year-round school, which meant that we went to school for six to eight weeks and then had two weeks off. I always thought that was a good system until we got to the summer.

Life was routine for our family during those days until one day when I was ten years old. Dad came home in an especially quiet mood. When we asked what was wrong, he said, "I got laid off."

I didn't understand what that really meant, so Mom explained to me that Dad could no longer work at Kelco, a company that was making products out of kelp. Upon learning that news, I tried to boost his spirits. "You'll find another job, Baba," I said, but at that age, I didn't understand how difficult that could be for a research chemist.

We had to cut our living expenses while Dad searched for another job. This meant eating a lot of fried rice with egg, diced scallions, and a slice of lunch ham chopped into small pieces. I knew things had become particularly tight when Mom and I got up at 4:30 A.M. to get ready for the flea market in Oceanside. No, we weren't going to buy but to sell. We tied old mattresses to the car roof and packed up the trunk and backseat with anything we could sell—books, clothes we had outgrown, household knickknacks, and old rackets.

Mom doesn't like to talk about the other job she took on while Dad was laid off—selling cemetery lots. To me, that shows the love she had for her family. My mom is a good saleswoman, but let's face it, how many people are dying to buy a cemetery lot? On top of that, she was trying to sell burial plots to Asians, and they never like to contemplate what happens when they die.

That shows how special my mom is. She also tried to sell different items—health foods and Chinese jackets made of soft material that reached to thigh level. Instead of buttons, the jackets closed with a loop and ball of material. She sold those Chinese jackets to friends and folks she ran into—even a few of my teachers. Mom would not sit around the house waiting for government assistance to arrive in the form of a check.

She also displayed incredible resilience in the face of personal adversity. A couple of years after we moved to La Costa, thieves broke into our home and robbed our valuables again! This time they also stole 8-millimeter films of Carl and me playing tennis. As the years pass by, those missing films have become priceless to us.

I remember hearing that our house was one of several in the neighborhood that were robbed. A couple of days after the break-in, Carl and I were walking to the bus stop. We saw a car parked on the other side with four guys sitting inside, killing time.

After a few minutes, we watched the four men exit the car and approach a house. This was in broad daylight.

Carl and I caught our bus before the men returned, but I can remember the license plate to this day—849 HOW.

We should have called the police, but we never did, probably because Carl and I were too young and naive to figure out what was happening.

CHAPTER 4

JUNIOR TENNIS DAYS

The journey from playing Nerf ball in a Minnesota basement to Court Central at Roland Garros took ten years and thousands of hours of practice. Yet never once did I feel forced by my parents to play tennis. Carl and I were willing participants, and if anything, we saw firsthand how my parents scrimped here and saved a dollar there if it could pay for our considerable tournament entry fees or reserve another lesson with a pro. Later on, junior tennis became *really* expensive when we began competing in national tournaments in Orlando, Houston, and Kalamazoo, Michigan. Mom and Dad somehow paid the mountainous bills through tight-fisted frugality, a trait that I inherited. Now I understand why I can never remember my folks taking any kind of vacation for themselves. Everything they did was for Carl's and my benefit.

Stepping into the cauldron of Southern California junior tennis was an eye-opening experience for all of us. Not only was the level of competition leagues above Minneapolis-Saint Paul, but you had to deal with the whole "juniors" scene. That included long drives to tournament sites, long waits to play your matches, inevitable squabbles with opponents on the other side of the net, and a few (but not as bad as today) pushy "tennis parents" who walked around with dollar signs and Wimbledon titles in their eyes.

Junior tennis is not like Little League baseball, where an umpire calls the balls and strikes and generally runs the game while ignoring the hooting and hollering from parents and coaches. In junior tennis, the youthful players are responsible for calling the lines on their sides of the court. There are no umpires. That is, until you get sick and tired of questionable calls and you request a line judge. Parents are supposed to sit away from the court and just watch, but the temptation to get involved or coach often proves too tempting. Coaching during matches is against the rules, unless the players split sets and take a ten-minute rest break.

I soon learned that if I did not stick up for myself, I would get "hooked" by character-challenged players with reputations for calling "tight" lines at crunch time. It didn't help matters that I continued to be height-challenged in those days; I didn't break the five-foot barrier until I was eleven. That didn't keep me from "playing up" in the Boys 12 or even the Boys 14 events against stronger—and considerably taller—players. I'm sure more than a few took their measure of me and decided I was someone who wouldn't stand up to a bad call or would let them win because they were bigger or ranked higher than me.

They were wrong. I was pretty feisty on the tennis court, even if I looked like a shrimp to them. I remember playing against an older guy named Tom Blackmore, who was ranked No. 1 in Southern California in his age group. We were having a tough match, and then I made a close call against him.

"You called that ball out!?" yelled Tom as he approached the net. "Are you sure that ball was out?" Tom was trying to bully me.

I turned around and faced my adversary. "That ball was O-U-T out!"

I stood up for my calls because I knew they were fair. I wasn't going to back down. When words were exchanged, I stood my ground. When someone beat me, I couldn't wait until tomorrow to play him again. Losing instilled a greater fighting spirit in me.

One time I lost to a kid named Mike who was two years older and ten inches taller than me. I didn't think he should have won that day, so I was upset. I went behind the locker room and cried a little bit. Then I got mad. I ran into his older brother and told him to deliver a message: "You tell Mike that the next time we play, I'm going to beat him." That's how I felt. When you're ten years old, tennis matches are life and death, and I hated to lose.

Hitting Two-on-One

My days fell into a routine. I got up, walked to school, learned my three R's, and walked home, where I would scramble for anything good to eat. Carl and I would change quickly into our tennis clothes so Mom could drive us to our club to practice, play practice sets, or take a lesson from the club pro. When Dad got off work, he would meet us at the club to check out how things were going.

On days when we didn't have anything organized at the club, Carl and I would usually watch a bit of TV before playing some mini-tennis in the backyard and doing some homework. Then Dad would pull into the driveway and take us to our club, where he would put Carl and me through various drills he had picked up from books or magazines. We hit the same shot over and over until Dad said we got it right. Playing with Dad was never drudgery. While he was workmanlike in his coaching approach, Dad encouraged us and tried to keep the drills moving so we never got bogged down. We didn't mind playing into the early evening and having a late dinner when we arrived home.

We did a lot of two-on-one hitting. For instance, I would hit ground strokes from the baseline, while Dad and Carl volleyed balls back from the net. Dad spent much of his time coaching us *how* to hit the ball properly. He was a great believer in having good strokes. Because Dad built our strokes, he learned how to fine-tune and fix them when we began spraying shots outside the lines. We became the player output of his instructional input.

It would be easy to say that my father, a research chemist by day, oversaw an after-hours tennis laboratory with his two sons as lab specimens. It really wasn't like that, although he often said that tennis is a lot like chemistry—an amalgamation of one part physical and two parts discipline and consistency. Dad worked with the material on hand, which is why Carl and I became vastly different players.

Because of my petite size and quickness, I became an offensive counterpunch-type player, mainly because I was usually pitted against bigger, stronger opponents. I took their best shots and whacked them back faster and deeper. If my opponent was a steady player, however, I adopted a slower-paced approach and moved my adversary from corner to corner. Carl, who was bulkier and barrel-chested, didn't like to play that way. He preferred to blow people off the court by crunching his serve and backing that up with big ground strokes and put-away volleys. He knew one speed—all out—and that playing approach worked

for him. Since each style matched up with our physiques and tempera-
ments, Dad was wise to work within our gifts and abilities. I think he
saw tennis as a path to college scholarships for his sons, but that was as
far as it went in the early years.

Quite frankly, Carl and I could not get enough of the game. I even
wore my tennis warm-ups to school because I couldn't wait to put a
racket in my hand once the final bell rang. After school or after dinner
or on weekends when we didn't have a tournament, Carl and I played
mini-tennis or "dink-em" on the cement patio in our backyard. We tied
a string from one patio post to another; then Carl grabbed a bedsheet
and draped it over the string to complete our net. The singles court
lines were defined by red bricks in the patio cement.

Our backyard court was fairly good-sized—maybe twelve or fifteen
feet long. We played with a regular ball and racket, but you had to bunt
each shot. You could not overhit, or you automatically lost the point.
(This rule was the source of many Cain-and-Abel arguments.) You
could rush the bedsheet net, but again, no overhitting.

Matches were often best-of-five sets, although sometimes we played
two-of-three. For variety, we strung up our bedsheet net on the backyard grass for a session of grass court tennis. The grass wasn't exactly
playable since every bounce was either a bad one or not one at all—but
it still made for a good cushion when we fell. We needed a grass court
because Wimbledon and the Australian Open were played on grass in
those days. (The Australian Open didn't switch to Rebound Ace—a
rubberized hard court—until 1988.) We even painted white lines with
spray paint.

Playing on grass was fun! We dived for balls and pretended we were
McEnroe making a stab volley on Centre Court. Because the ball

bounced so badly on the grass, we often chipped and charged to volley before the ball hit the ground.

Our backyard tennis wars continued into junior high. I remember playing in Houston in a national clay court tournament and bringing home a brown grocery bag full of green particles of clay. Carl and I spread the green Har-Tru dirt over our patio floor and pretended we were playing Roland Garros.

We did many things in that backyard besides play tennis. We played baseball with a regular tennis ball. Ground ball was a single. Ice plant was a double. Hitting the fence was a triple, and over the fence was a home run.

One time when I was pitching, I looked in for the sign, then went into an exaggerated, slow windup while I pitched the tennis ball straight down the pipe. Carl swung hard, nailed my offering—and smacked me in the forehead even though I was wearing a hat! I never saw the ball because it shot off his bat so fast.

Carl laughed his head off, and after a while I had to admit it was funny that a tennis ball struck me right between the eyes. Fortunately, it *was* a tennis ball. I remember watching a baseball game and seeing one of the batters get plunked in the head from a pitch by a hardball. After that, I never had a desire to play Little League baseball.

I did play some soccer, however, and even played on a team with Carl—with Dad as the coach. Although soccer was fun, I preferred the self-reliance of tennis—not having to rely on any teammates to win a match or come from behind. Tennis demanded mental toughness, playing under pressure, hitting the big shot on the big point, making one more get, and keeping the heat on even when things weren't going so well. All those aspects appealed to me. I was learning that size and strength were not the determining factors in tennis—it was heart.

BIG BROTHER PAVES THE WAY

Carl was the first Chang to make a name in junior tennis. He earned a U.S. national ranking before me, and by the time he reached high school, he was one of the best in San Diego junior tennis. Carl played in the same age-group as Andre Agassi, and I can remember Carl taking Andre down, 6–0, 6–1, at the Fiesta Bowl Boys 14s. I can't recall Carl ever losing to Pete Sampras in the juniors.

It helped having a big brother who was a better player—I always had someone good to practice with. Sibling rivalry had never existed between Carl and me, although we had a running bet going on between us. We saw each other as friends and allies, rather than brotherly rivals, except for the times we flung pillows at each other. Playing with Carl is why I improved so much in my first few years of tennis, and spending so much time on the court together brought us closer. Then again, we had grown up doing *everything* together, on and off the court.

Not long after we moved to La Costa, we got up before sunrise and walked two miles to the La Costa golf course with fishing poles in hand. Some buddies in the neighborhood were waiting for us.

"Here, this way," said the ringleader. "Follow me."

"Are you sure it's okay?" I asked, perhaps a little late.

"As long as the ranger doesn't get you," he said. "If he catches you fishing on the golf course, he takes your pole and calls your parents." Apparently, La Costa had some prized Japanese koi in their ponds, as well as some stocked largemouth bass.

Everything seemed spooky to Carl and me because it was still dark when we found the small pond next to one of the greens. We baited our hooks and started fishing.

The first half hour, we caught several bass. Then out of nowhere, a ranger popped out of the woods, looking every inch an authority figure.

"What are you boys doing here?" he bellowed.

No one said a word. No one took a step.

"You boys oughtn't be fishing here. This is a golf course, and fishing is forbidden."

One of the kids was brave—or maybe he didn't want to lose his fishing pole.

"Do you know Ranger John?" he asked.

"No, I believe I don't," replied the gruff-looking superintendent.

"The last time we were here, he said we could fish this pond as long as we were gone before the golfers arrived."

All us kids knew he was lying, but we wished upon a star that this ranger would buy the story.

"Well, you're not supposed to fish here, even before the golfers come through," he said. "Tell you what. If you kids hightail it out of here, I won't march you back to the clubhouse."

We were gone in thirty seconds, but that didn't stop Carl and me from making other clandestine early morning visits. One time Carl was rewarded with a huge, five-pound bass, and I caught my share of pan-sized bass.

The two of us were also catching our share of junior tournament titles. I would say that I was around ten years old when I had won nearly everything from Santa Barbara to the Mexican border. We still couldn't afford for me to travel to national tournaments, but fortunately the Boys 12 hard courts were played practically in my backyard—Morley Field in San Diego's Balboa Park—making it a cheap tournament to play.

I remember playing the Boys 12 in the summer of 1982 when I was ten years old. There was another player in the draw—Andre Agassi, who was twelve. Andre stayed at our house, and when we showed up at Morley Field a day before the tournament, we ran to have a look at the draw.

"I'm going to play the top seed in the quarters," Andre announced as he pointed to the draw sheet.

"Quarters? You have to beat me in the third round first!" I said, mustering all the bravado I could as a ten-year-old. I wanted to make sure that Andre didn't overlook me.

We did rendezvous in the third round. Back in those days, Andre liked to hit everything with a lot of crazy spin—severe underspin off backhand approaches, exaggerated topspin off his forehand, and an "American twist" on his serve. In our match, he even served *underhand* to me. His underhand serve had such unbelievable sidespin that it broke four feet off to the side after it bounced in the service court.

Andre won, as expected, but I returned the following year to Morley Field, where I marched all the way to the finals before losing to Fritz Bissell of Des Moines, Iowa. A year later in my final year in the Boys 12, I still hadn't hit my growth spurt (I stood just five-feet, one-inch tall and weighed ninety pounds), but I defeated Michael Flanagan of Dallas in the finals for my first national crown.

Winning a national tournament opened up all sorts of avenues for my tennis. I was invited to attend the U.S. Tennis Association's training camp in New York City, and suddenly I *had* to play various national-level tournaments around the country. Meanwhile, Carl qualified to play national tournaments as well, but our traveling costs stretched my parents' budget to the limit.

Mom and Dad gulped and borrowed money against the house in 1985 by refinancing. They were spending more than twenty thousand dollars a year—an astronomical sum for them—on airfares, hotels, restaurants, entry fees, rackets, strings, clothes, and shoes. We were a one-income family, except when Mom's odd jobs brought in a few dollars. Bottom line: we didn't have the bucks to compete against the country club kids. We had the collective will to find a way, however.

Dad purchased a Winn stringing machine so we could string our own rackets. We stayed at Motel 6 at out-of-town tournaments since it was cheap but pretty clean. Carl and I always got the beds, which meant that my parents sacrificially took the floor or even the bathtub at bedtime.

We also spent the night at friends' homes in the Los Angeles area and accepted free housing organized by the tournament. My parents appreciated how tennis-minded families opened their homes and their refrigerators to us. (We returned the favor as well. Andre Agassi was just one of many juniors who stayed at our home during tournaments.)

Our family also benefited from other people's largesse. When Pancho Segura heard about these two Chang kids kicking up a storm, he invited Carl and me to drop by La Costa so that the legendary teacher could "look over" our games. Pancho knew the situation: we couldn't afford his customary hourly rate. But he gave freely of himself and provided countless pointers, never charging us a dime. I'll never forget his insights or his generosity.

AN EIGHTH GRADER AMONG SENIORS

In the fall of 1985, Dad was looking at all angles to get as much competition for me as he could. *Why not play high school tennis?* he thought.

There was this little problem: I was still an eighth grader at Oak Crest Junior High in Encinitas. Even worse, Oak Crest was a seventh-through-ninth-grade junior high, so I would have to wait *two* years before I could play at San Dieguito High (now San Dieguito Academy), the Encinitas high school where Carl was an eleventh grader.

Dad called Kendall Webb, the San Diego CIF (California Interscholastic Federation) commissioner, and learned that if I took at least one high school–level class while I was in eighth grade, I would qualify to play on the San Dieguito High team. The trade-off was that I would have to relinquish my senior year eligibility in tennis, however.

I didn't know that I would win the French Open in what would have been my junior year of high school, but Dad thought that playing high school tennis in the eighth grade sounded like a wonderful idea. I did too. I could play side by side with Carl in a low-pressure team atmosphere, as compared to the cutthroat competition found in junior tennis. That fall, I enrolled in a ninth-grade Algebra 1 honors class given at Oak Crest, which qualified me to play for San Dieguito High.

Carl and I had a blast playing together. Our coach was Larry Mulvania, who didn't mind two Asian-American kids strategizing with him about the lineup. We helped the coach, well, *coach,* and we even drilled some of the other players. Our big rival was Vista High, whose team was filled with nationally ranked players from a nearby tennis academy. Carl and I informed Coach Larry that if I won all three of my singles matches and matched Carl with Andy Lee in doubles, Carl could carry him and win all three doubles sets. And if Ed Chin played doubles with . . .

We had it all figured out. Coach Larry listened and went with our lineup—but we came up a little bit short even though Carl and I won all our matches. Vista High was our only blemish in 1986. We had a great time being part of the San Dieguito team. Coach Larry wasn't autocratic like some coaches, who said if you missed practice you couldn't play. Sometimes we *had* to skip practice because we had a tournament or a hitting session with a top-notch player. But most of the time Carl and I practiced with each other or participated in team drills.

After one Chang-devised lineup beat another rival team, Coach Larry said, "That was great, guys. Tell you what. My treat today. We'll stop for hamburgers on the way home, and you can order all you want."

Like most kids on the team, Carl and I rarely had more than a few dollars in our pockets, so we greeted this invitation with enthusiasm. Coach Larry drove us posthaste to the 29¢ Hamburger Store, where hamburgers were really cheap—twenty-nine cents. You could call it a poor man's version of White Castle. I ordered four burgers and a bag of fries, just like my buddies. I had to keep up. But those hamburgers were good going down and bad once they got there! Twenty minutes later, while in Coach's car, I got sick as a dog. All the guys were moaning because they felt they were about to throw up as well.

At the end of the season, we had the Palomar League Championships. Since Carl and I hadn't lost a set all season, we were seeded one and two, respectively. We advanced to the finals, which caused a lot of interest. Brother against brother. Eighth grader against high school junior. Carl's classmates sat at one end of the cement seats at our home club—the Cardiff Courts Racquet Club (now the Bobby Riggs Tennis Center)—while my friends, most of whom had arrived on skateboards, sat at the other.

Since Carl was seventeen and I was fourteen, there was quite an age gap in terms of physical strength and maturity. Carl and I had played six times over the years in junior tournaments, but he had bested me every time.

I felt good playing against Carl because I knew what to expect. We mixed it up from the first point, and for three hours and fifteen minutes, we fought and fought until I beat my brother for the first time: 7–6, 4–6, 7–6. Carl teased me by saying that the smarter, faster, and uglier player won.

But that nip-and-tuck match was an hors d'oeuvre compared to the San Diego CIF Championships a week later, which brought together all the top high school players in San Diego County. Once again Carl and I marched to the finals, and the match we played at the Bishop's School in La Jolla turned out to be déjà vu all over again. It all came down to a third-set tiebreaker for the second week in a row, but this time Carl staked out a 4–1 lead. My big brother let down his guard just a little bit, however, and I stormed back to win the tiebreaker 9–7 and the match 6–4, 3–6, 7–6. I believe I became the youngest player in San Diego history to win the CIF Championship.

During the match, I must have frustrated my brother, because at one point he threw up his hands and shouted across the net, "When are you going to turn pro?"

In eighteen months, as it turned out.

THE NEXT ROUND

I was finally going through my growth spurt, sprouting up to five-feet, six-and-a-half inches (I've got to include that half-inch), but I was still playing against taller players who were starting to shave. During the summer of 1986, I was invited to try out for the U.S. Junior Davis Cup team, the elite squad of junior players. I qualified, making me the youngest player on a team filled with seventeen- and eighteen-year-olds.

The competition was steep; Pete Sampras tried out and didn't make the final cut. Once you were on the team, the USTA paid for all your summertime travel, including room and board, and they sent us to international tournaments. Not only did the Junior Davis Cup ease the financial pressure on my parents' shoulders, but it was viewed as a stepping-stone to greater things, another rung up the ladder to topflight international competition.

Jim Courier, a redhead from Florida, and I were matched as roommates. I don't remember if he was wearing those famous tube socks in those days, but his fair skin seemed to dry up continually, so he was constantly borrowing lotion from me. We got along well.

That summer I played Jim at the U.S. National 16s, which is held every August in Kalamazoo, Michigan. It's the most important—and prestigious—junior tournament on the calendar, and we both wanted to do well. We were deep into the third set on a hot afternoon when Jim began cramping. A few points later he cramped so badly that he keeled over onto the court and had to default to me.

After the match, I offered him some potassium chloride. "It'll help you with the cramps," I said.

"Sure, now you offer them to me, after I defaulted," said Jim. "Thanks a lot." Jim was laughing when he said it.

When I was fourteen, I wore Fila clothes and Reebok shoes on the court. I had liked the way Fila clothes looked ever since I saw Bjorn Borg wear those pinstripe shirts when he won Wimbledon five straight times in the late 1970s. As for the Reebok sneakers, I thought they were more classic than Nike, which everyone seemed to be talking about since some basketball player named Michael Jordan had introduced sneakers called "Air Jordans." The tennis Nikes, however, were an ugly gray and white, and I didn't like them. As for my racket, I was very pleased with the Prince Graphite 110, an oversize frame.

At the end of the summer, Dad felt that the Junior Davis Cup team didn't help me to improve as much as I should have, although he greatly appreciated the relief on the family finances. As we mapped out a strategy for 1987, he wanted me to concentrate on winning the U.S. National 18s—a tall order for someone fifteen years old. We both knew there was an ulterior motive: win the U.S. Nationals, and you pocket an automatic invitation to the U.S. Open three weeks later in New York City. Dad felt that playing the U.S. Open would be a great experience for me, if I was fortunate enough to win Kalamazoo.

When I reached the 1987 U.S. National 18s semifinals, Al Parker was waiting to play me. Al was the No. 1–ranked junior in the country and had won more national titles than any boy in the history of junior tennis. He was the clear odds-on favorite. Experience was on his side since he had just graduated from high school.

On the morning of the match, a series of thunderstorms swept through Kalamazoo. Our match would have to be moved indoors.

"Michael, I've got some advice for you." It was Carl, who had lost to Al in the second round.

Although I was eager to hear his advice, I eyed Carl warily. Earlier in the week, I had gone to a "Supercuts" in Kalamazoo—and I got a supercut all right. It was a chop—a really bad haircut! The woman with the scissors must have been in a bad mood since my hair looked like she had taken out her troubles on me. We're talking about a *bad* haircut— white sidewalls and uneven all around. I remember walking out of Supercuts, only to be greeted by the sound of Carl's laughter.

"Mommy, make him stop!"

"Ooh, that's a brutal butchering you got there," said Carl. "I want a picture of that."

"Forget it, Carl. Mommy, can you tell him to stop picking on me?"

Carl was laughing so hard that he was holding his sides. "Where did she find the bowl?" he asked.

"Mommy . . ."

"Did you give her a tip?" Carl asked.

"Well . . . yeah."

Then Mom started laughing.

"But, Mommy . . ."

"Well, it will grow back," she offered.

Now Carl wanted to share some advice about my upcoming match with Al Parker.

"What do you think I should do?" I asked.

"You should go into the indoor courts early to get your eyes adjusted."

"Why?"

"See how bright it is out here? It's dark inside. Your eyes need time to adjust."

Carl's advice made sense to me, so I grabbed my racket bag and walked into the indoor tennis hall and sat on the bench next to our court for fifteen minutes. I tried not to think too much and to just settle my nerves.

Kalamazoo usually draws crowds of a thousand or more to its outdoor matches, but there weren't any grandstands indoors. The tournament committee decided to put us on an indoor court flanked by courts on either side. The hundreds of spectators had to stand to watch the match. It felt a bit claustrophobic having so many people stand on both sides of the court.

I don't remember if I got off to a quick start, but I do know that I didn't get off to a slow start against Al. At one point toward the end of the first set, Al hit a winner on an important point against me. He pumped his fist at me and screamed, "Yeaah!" while he shot a look at me.

It was a challenge. I walked toward the net and screamed, "Do it, Al. Do it!"

Everyone froze. I don't know why I said that, but it had to be the heat of the moment. I guess I wanted to show him I could match emotion with emotion—stand my ground with him. Tennis has been compared to boxing, and although you never touch your opponent, you try to inflict wounds by bludgeoning the ball and staying mentally strong. You never give your opponent an inch or an inkling he can beat you. If Al was going to pump his fist in my face, I was going to fight back. I think I picked up that personality trait from Mom, who always rose to our defense when she saw her sons getting a raw deal.

I upset Al Parker that day, 6–4, 6–4, but waiting for me in the finals was none other than Jim Courier. This time, I was sure he was carrying potassium chloride in his bag.

On the morning of the finals for the U.S. National 18s, Dad had to fly back home. He had purchased a nonrefundable ticket, and the airlines were inflexible. He *had* to be on that Sunday noontime flight. (It wasn't all for naught: Dad watched the end of the match in the airport lounge, since it was televised locally.) Before he left that morning, he gave me a pep talk and some strategy. "Jim's going to hit hard, so your strategy is to offensive counterpunch and use his power."

"Right, Baba."

The weather was holding, but the forecast called for more thunderstorms. The tournament committee, headed by the USTA president,

David Markin, didn't want to play such an important match indoors. Plus, there was no way they could seat anybody.

"Michael, we're not going to play best-of-five sets today because of the weather forecast," said Mr. Markin. "It's going to be two-out-of-three."

The finals of the U.S. Nationals had always been best-of-five. I figured the longer the match, the better my chances that Jim would cramp up as he had the previous year.

"I'd rather play best-of-five, Mr. Markin. Isn't the weather going to hold?"

"No, we can't take that chance," said the USTA president. "If we don't finish and get this match completed, that's not good. A lot of people have planes to catch."

I played really well, took Jim's considerable power and used it against him, and won 6–4, 6–2 and a wild-card entry into the U.S. Open.

I was going to Flushing Meadow.

TUNE-UP TIME

Only three weeks passed between Kalamazoo and the U.S. Open—more than enough time to get excited about the prospect of playing on the world stage. Maybe I would play McEnroe or Lendl or Wilander or Becker. Wouldn't that be awesome?

Fortunately, I had gotten my feet wet in the pro game a few weeks before Kalamazoo when Carl, Mom, and I traveled to Lawrence, Kansas, for a USTA satellite tournament. This was tennis's minor league—the real entry-level for our sport. Since Carl and I didn't have any ATP points, we were relegated to the qualification draws just to get *into* the satellite tournament. The "qualies," as we called them, were populated with testosterone-rich college players, guys carrying big racket bags who strutted their stuff about the grounds. The qualification tournament draw was filled with 256 players; win five rounds, and you'd be among the final eight who qualified for the main draw of the satellite tournament. Once in the main draw, you were playing guys with world rankings as high as the top 300.

I won my five rounds in the qualies, then fought my way to the semi-finals in the main draw, which raised a few eyebrows since the players were so much older than me. Then I learned that I didn't get to keep my ATP points because I wasn't playing all the legs of the satellite tour. Still, it was a great experience.

After Kalamazoo, Mom and I traveled to New York a week before the U.S. Open. I had received a wild card to play in a tune-up event at Rye Brook, New York. Before the tournament started, we dropped by the club to find someone to practice with.

I approached the tournament desk. "Excuse me," I began. "Would there be anyone I can practice with?"

"Well, you can go out to the practice courts and see if you can find anyone," said the woman behind the desk.

I approached the practice courts like a kindergartner approaches the first day of school—with great trepidation. No one knew me. Who would want to play with a fifteen-year-old? I felt painfully shy and awkward in those days.

The courts were deserted except for one where a couple of South American guys were blasting balls back and forth. I stood off to the side and watched.

The players' coach noticed me standing by myself. He walked over and thrust out his hand. "Hi, I'm Colon Nunez. Do you have someone to hit with?"

"No." I tried to rack my brain, asking where I had heard this name. Colon looked to be in his late twenties and spoke good English, although I could tell that Spanish was his native tongue.

"Well, let's hit some."

We didn't trade groundies for more than two minutes when he started coaching *me*. "How come you're hitting like that?" he asked. "Why aren't you moving your feet?"

I got with the program in a hurry. After about forty-five minutes of heavy-duty ball striking, he motioned me to come up to the net. "This is what I'll do for you," said Colon. "You can train with us for the rest of the week and also through the Open. I'll take care of you for practice."

After I lost to Jim Pugh in the first round at Rye Brook, I practiced for nearly two weeks with the players Colon was coaching: Andres Gomez from Ecuador, Jaime Yzaga from Peru, and Tarik Benhabiles from France. I trained and played practice sets all day long, and Colon never asked to be paid.

A few days before the U.S. Open, Mom and I received a phone call from Dad, who was back in California.

"The U.S. Open draw just came out!" Dad exclaimed.

"Who do I play?"

"You play Paul Mac-nam-ee." That's the way he said it.

"Who?"

"Paul Mac-nam-ee."

I had never heard of him. Then a light went on. "Oh, you mean Paul McNamee," I said, pronouncing the last name Mack-na-mee. "Baba, your pronunciation is terrible," I teased.

I didn't know much about Paul McNamee except that he was a veteran player from Australia who had changed from a one-handed backhand to a two-handed backhand in the middle of his pro career. No one had ever heard of a touring pro successfully retooling his game that radically, but apparently Paul had been able to pull it off. He was thirty-two years old—seventeen years my senior.

If you had seen me play that opening-round match at the U.S. Tennis Center, you would have thought that I would play the rest of my career as a serve-and-volleyer. I came in behind my serve quite a few times that afternoon because I had noticed that Paul was having a tough time returning kick serves high to his backhand. Each time I kicked the ball in deep to his backhand, he floated his return, which I knocked off for a volley winner. That strategy helped me to win in four sets. Beating Paul McNamee at fifteen made me the youngest male to ever win a match in the Open era.

I was suddenly a *story*. Reporters rushed me like fans rushing a stage at a rock concert, and I was overwhelmed. I think I developed a bad case of stage fright because I don't remember being very articulate. Fans followed me around the U.S. Tennis Center like I was the pied piper, and kids—and adults—were asking me for my autograph. Now *that* felt funny.

I'm sure that Paul endured a round of ribbing in the locker room for losing to a kid still in junior high. Now that some years have passed since that event, I run into guys who lost to me when I was fifteen, sixteen, and seventeen years old, and they seemed to wear that defeat like a badge of honor. "Yeah, I lost to you when you were fifteen," one will say with a sheepish grin. They are actually quite proud of it, although at the time they must have hated losing to a kid.

In round two, I played on an outside court against Nduko Odizor, a twenty-nine-year-old black player from Nigeria. Sitting off to the side of court 16 were U.S. Davis Cup captain Tom Gorman and former players Arthur Ashe and Brian Gottfried, who wanted an up-close-and-personal look at this Asian-American kid causing all the hoopla. The press were giving me tons of coverage because no American male player had won a Grand Slam since John McEnroe captured the 1984 U.S. Open, and they loved to speculate who the Next Great Hope would be.

There was no way that Nduko would lose to a youngster, so he blasted quickly out of the blocks by winning the first two sets, 6–1, 6–2. I had been there before—in the basement back in Minnesota. I fought my way into the match and won the next two sets. Serving at 3–4 in the fifth set, it was a critical juncture—15–30. Nduko chipped and charged, but I hit a good passing shot. Nduko, stretching at full extension, popped up a short ball. I ran in and had plenty of time to put the ball away, but Nduko charged the net, ducked, and waved his racket to distract me.

I got distracted, all right. I looked up and hit my shot long. Nduko went on to break me and serve out the match, 6–3.

I had committed a rookie mistake, but now I had a handful of ATP points in my racket bag (from Rye Brook and the U.S. Open), which converted into a world ranking of 920.

I was on my way.

A BILLBOARD ACT

The notoriety of winning a match at the U.S. Open opened up all sorts of avenues. In the fall of 1987, I received wild cards to play in the Las Vegas Challenger (a minor league tournament) and Scottsdale (a major league ATP tournament). For Las Vegas, Mom and I checked into the King 8 motel just off the Strip. We soon learned that the King 8, which had inexpensive room rates, attracted a rougher crowd. The Friday before we checked in, someone had been murdered at the motel. Then Mom asked for new sheets because it looked like housekeeping hadn't changed them in the last hour, if you catch my drift.

When I kept winning in Las Vegas, Dad drove over from San Diego to watch me play. When he took one look at the King 8, he announced, "You can't stay here. Let's go to a nicer hotel."

Mom and I were in agreement with each other—and not with him. "Baba, we're winning in this hotel," I said. "We're *not* moving."

Good thing, because I won the Las Vegas Challenger.

Two weeks before at Scottsdale, a Phoenix suburb, I was playing against Ben Testerman in a first-round match when I started walking funny after a point. I looked down and saw the sole of my left shoe flip-flopping like a beach sandal. Bizarre!

I didn't have another pair of sneakers in my racket bag. What fifteen-year-old *would* carry an extra pair of tennis shoes around?

I turned around and motioned to my parents that my shoe was falling apart. At first they didn't believe me until I showed them.

"Try to keep playing while we try to find you some shoes," said Mom. Then she and Dad frantically began walking through the crowd, looking at people's shoes!

Mom spotted an older gentleman wearing some tennis shoes.

"Excuse me," said Mom, "but is that a size nine shoe you're wearing?"

"Uh, yeah," responded the gentleman with a puzzled look on his face.

"Could we borrow your shoes? You won't believe this, but Michael's shoes are falling apart and he needs a pair to finish this match."

"You're kidding, right?"

"No, really. Michael needs some tennis shoes!"

That brought a laugh from those watching this play out.

"Sure, here you go," said the man, who whipped off his tennis shoes and handed them to Mom.

I slipped into the borrowed sneakers on the next changeover and then finished off Ben. Scottsdale turned out to be a great tournament for me as I won three matches and became the youngest player ever to reach an ATP semifinal. Brad Gilbert, then ranked No. 13, stopped me 6–4, 6–4 in the semis, but I gave him some nervous moments along the way. My semifinal result paid twelve thousand dollars, which looked like a pot of gold to us, but I could not accept the prize money since I was still an amateur. I could be reimbursed for my expenses, however. Since I had twelve grand to work with, I figured there was more than enough to go around, so I went out and treated Colon Nunez to a round of golf after losing Saturday afternoon.

When it came time to present my expense sheet, the tournament committee examined it line by line. Two things caught their eye: two hundred dollars in greens fees and a rental car.

"Golf is not a legitimate expense, nor is a rental car because we provided player transportation," the tournament director informed me.

I was ticked that they didn't cover the golf since we played on the same site as the tournament. But the rental car? "My mother needed the car so she could go to the grocery store," I explained. Mom had been cooking chicken and noodles for me back at the hotel.

"No, we're not going to cover it." Mom, standing next to me, started crying. Four hundred dollars in added expenses nearly killed us at that time, but the tournament committee—actually, the Men's Tennis Council—stuck to their guns.

Oh, well. The bad news was that we were out a considerable sum of money, but the good news was that my world ranking now stood at 163.

Like a new record release on *Billboard,* you could put a bullet next to my name.

• MOM AND I USED TO PLANT TULIPS TOGETHER
WHEN I WAS A CHILD IN MINNESOTA.
HERE WE ENJOY THE TULIP FESTIVAL TOGETHER. •

——— • ———

CHAPTER 5

TAKING A DIFFERENT PATH

My world was changing rapidly in more ways than one when I was fifteen years old. Not only was my tennis world exploding before my eyes, but so was my world away from the tennis court. In moments when I lost myself in thought, I pondered the big questions of life: Who am I? What am I going to be? Do my friends like me? What will my future be like?

I didn't have any quick answers. Like many teens, I was caught in that awkward world between childhood and adulthood, with one foot planted in both camps. My life as a tennis player had certainly matured me, probably beyond my years, but deep inside, I was still a young boy in many ways.

I've heard it said that God plants these types of questions in every person's heart, and if that's true, I was certainly hearing them when I was fifteen years old. I had grown up hearing about a Supreme Being from my parents, who took Carl and me to a Chinese Christian church fairly regularly. The problem was that I had a negative attitude about church in general. I flat out didn't want to go, and I had felt that way for as long as I could remember. I dragged my feet as badly as any toe-dragging server.

This is how our Sunday mornings went on those weekends when we weren't playing in some junior tournament. Mom and Dad would drag Carl and me out of bed and then announce that we were going to church at nine o'clock.

"Oh, Mommy, do we have to?" I whined. I never greeted this news with enthusiasm.

"Yes, we do," she replied. "And I don't want any excuses."

Since I didn't want to go to church, I tried to do everything in my power to keep us from going. My best bet was to stall. Mom always insisted on a Sunday morning bath, but if I soaked for a long, long time (by constantly demanding more hot water), dressed in slow motion, and ate my fried rice v-e-r-y slowly, chances were better than fifty-fifty that we would be running too late to make it to the church on time. That's when my parents would throw up their hands and say, "Okay, next week."

If foot-dragging didn't work, I could always resort to the "Can we watch church on TV?" ploy. That gambit worked several times, which was great since anything was better than sitting in a boring church. Why did I have such a negative attitude? Because I was an ants-in-my-pants type of boy. I fussed and fidgeted in the church pew while the pastor droned on and on. He seemed to talk forever.

Mom and Dad would have put me in Sunday school, where I could have sat on the floor with my peers and listened to Bible stories and completed craft projects, but the church we attended didn't have a Sunday school. The only time I was put in Sunday school was when we visited my grandfather's church in Thousand Oaks. While seeing my cousins several times a year was always great, visiting Gohng-Gohng's church was a pain. I always felt "behind" in the Sunday school classroom. My cousins Jimmy, Joe, and Jerry seemed to raise their hands every time the teacher asked who Noah or Jonah or Moses was. I didn't understand anything they were talking about, so I clammed up and hoped the teacher would not call on me. I didn't want to get embarrassed.

When Carl and I were growing up, Mom and Dad took us to church because they thought it was important to instill some religious instruction in their children. I cannot recall discussions, however, where my parents explained what it was to have a personal relationship with Jesus Christ. We also did not have a family time for praying and studying the Bible, known as "devotions" in Christian circles.

We did have a big Bible in our house, but that was more for decoration. That ten-pound Bible, which looked to me like the heaviest book ever published, didn't look at all user-friendly, although it contained a few illustrations that I would look at from time to time. On a few occasions, Mom would sit with me and look at some of the pictures, but that didn't happen often.

However, don't get the wrong impression about Mom and Dad. My parents were very moral people, and they wanted to be sure their sons knew the difference between right and wrong. It's just that the Christian walk—which I'll explain more about later—isn't just about going to church and being a good person, as I was soon to discover.

RECEIVING AN INCREDIBLE GIFT

One time on a family visit to Thousand Oaks, "Ah-ma" (my term of endearment for my grandmother) gave me a Bible.

"Please read this every day," she said. "God has so much to teach you, and this Bible has notes that you can read."

"Sure, Ah-ma." I must have been fourteen years old at the time.

I surveyed the Bible she handed me.

"That's an *NIV Student Bible*," she explained. "NIV stands for New International Version."

"What's that?"

"That means the translation is into easy-to-read English. I think this Bible will be just right for you," said Ah-ma.

I thumbed through a few pages. I didn't see any of the "thee's" and "thou's" or other archaisms like the ones sprinkled through Dad's Bible, which I found incomprehensible. I could understand what I was reading in the *Student Bible*. The English was clear and natural.

"Thank you, Ah-ma. I promise I'll read this Bible."

But that's as far as it went. Despite my best intentions to read my new Bible, they would remain just that—good intentions. Upon my return to San Diego, I stacked the *Student Bible* on a bookshelf in my room and promptly forgot about it.

Six months after receiving the Bible, we traveled again to Thousand Oaks for a family visit. During the main service in the church sanctuary, an elderly lady named Aunt Betty gave the sermon. Normally, I would mentally ready myself for thirty or forty minutes of tedium, a time to let my mind go totally blank while the speaker did his or her thing. Something about Aunt Betty caused me to sit and listen, however.

Perhaps it was because she spoke without notes. Maybe it was the way she stood in front of us and spoke from her heart. She even told a joke to start things off, and her subsequent stories contained humor, which kept me listening.

I can still remember what Aunt Betty talked about. That morning, she emphasized that God has reasons for everything. Sometimes we don't understand His timing, and when that happens, we have to trust Him. To illustrate this point, she told a story about a family in China that was rushing to catch a ferry to another peninsula, where they lived.

The family knew they were running a little bit late, so they hustled to the boat dock. "Hurry, we're going to miss the boat!" said the father.

The family arrived just in time to watch the ferry join the rest of the harbor traffic. They had missed their boat, and now they would have to wait six hours for the next ride.

"How are we going to get home?" asked one of the teenage girls.

"Yes, why did this have to happen?" asked her brother.

Their parents could not provide the answers, but for the next six hours, they took turns grumbling about missing the ferry.

Finally, they were able to board the next ferry for the long journey home. When they arrived at their destination, they noticed a big commotion around the dock area. They saw hundreds of people storming a small office, trying to push their way through the front door.

"What happened?" asked one of the family members.

"Didn't you hear?" replied someone. "The ferry sank, and there are no survivors."

Aunt Betty said there would be times when we don't understand what is happening in life, but one thing we can understand is that God is in control—He understands everything about us and our lives, and He knows what He is doing. "That family was humbled when they learned why God allowed them to miss that first boat," she said.

Aunt Betty's summation hit me like a thunderclap, and the story of the Chinese family that had missed the doomed ferry continued to resonate with me when I returned to school. A few days later, I was lying in bed, looking for something to do. I glanced over at my bookshelf and saw the *Student Bible* that Ah-ma had given me six months earlier.

Well, I wonder what the Bible has to say.

I had always learned that it was best to start reading a book at the beginning, so I thumbed through the Table of Contents and the Index. Then I began poking around my *Student Bible*, learning more of what God had to say on a variety of topics. I also read the four Gospels—Matthew, Mark, Luke, and John—from end to end and learned more about Jesus and how His love for me was so great that He died a gruesome death on a cross so that I might have eternal life with Him. No matter what happened, Christ would never forsake me or let me down.

Each page of my *Student Bible* contained one or two thought-provoking lessons, and every five or ten pages contained a longer reading that amplified a section of Scripture. For instance, I read in Mark 4 about the time Jesus went on a boat with his disciples one evening, and a furious squall came up and waves started breaking over the boat. The disciples feared for their lives and were sure they would perish. They woke Jesus up and asked, "Teacher, don't You care if we drown?"

That's when Jesus stood up and rebuked the wind and said to the waves, "Quiet! Be still!" The wind died, and the lake became completely calm again. Jesus said to His followers, "Why are you so afraid? Do you still have no faith?"

The disciples were terrified and asked each other, "Who is this? Even the wind and the waves obey Him!"

The *Student Bible* had this to say about Jesus calming the waters in the midst of a squall:

> American radio broadcaster Paul Harvey once told a modern parable about a religious skeptic who worked as a farmer. One raw winter night, the man heard an irregular thumping sound against the kitchen storm door. He went to a window and watched as tiny, shivering sparrows, attracted to the warmth inside, beat in vain against the glass. Touched, the farmer bundled up and trudged through fresh snow to open the barn door for the struggling birds. He turned on the lights and tossed some hay in the corner. But the sparrows, which had scattered in all directions when he emerged from the house, hid in the darkness, afraid.
>
> The man tried various tactics to get them into the barn. He laid down a trail of saltine cracker crumbs to direct them. He tried circling behind the barn to drive them toward the barn. Nothing worked. He, a huge alien creature, had terrified them; the birds couldn't comprehend that he actually desired to help them.
>
> The farmer withdrew to his house and watched the doomed

sparrows through a window. As he stared, a thought hit him like lightning from a clear blue sky. *If only I could become like a bird—one of them—just for a moment. Then I wouldn't frighten them so. I could show them warmth and safety.* At that time, another thought dawned on him. He had grasped the reason why Jesus was born.

I felt everything I read in my *Student Bible* was very true and right. I was learning how God wanted me to live my life. *This is cool,* I thought. *It would be cool to live my life as a Christian.*

And so in a quiet moment I prayed and asked Jesus to come into my heart, to change me according to His purposes. I can't tell you what day I officially became a Christian, but you know what? That's not important. What happened is that I reached a point where I knew who God was and that He was exactly who He said He was. If I believed in Jesus, I would have eternal life with Him. He would take me right where I was in life. I decided that I would follow Him and learn more about Him.

People may wonder if becoming a Christian had any effect on my tennis. No, nothing changed there. But I do think I experienced dramatic changes in how I acted as a person. I became more conscious of hurting people's feelings. I developed a greater conviction of what was right or what was wrong. I looked for ways to say kinder words, especially to my parents.

The subtle yet unmistakable changes in my personality did not escape Mom and Dad. Their son had changed, and it was because of the power of Jesus Christ to change people's lives. In their book, I was exhibit 1-A, and they were watching their son very closely.

• U.S. OPEN 1991 •

———— • ————

CHAPTER 6

PATHWAY TO THE PROS

After my surprising U.S. Open debut and semifinal finish in Scottsdale, I was the highest-ranked amateur player in the world—No. 163. What would happen next became the subject of family conversation over the next few months.

Much of our family interaction happened around the kitchen or dining room table. Eating and talking were important pastimes to our family, and had been ever since I had left my high chair. My parents saw the family dinner hour as a time to reconnect and share what happened during the day, discussing what happened in school or how things went on the tennis court—or both. They recognized that their sons needed a forum where we could express our dreams, our irrational fears, and our crazy ideas. Our commitment to eat together was why Mom always waited until everyone returned home from our evening workout session before serving dinner, even if it was after eight o'clock.

Mom's homemade dishes certainly put us in a talking mood. Mom cooked great Chinese food—as well as the occasional American meal (meatloaf, steak, or even fresh homemade bread). It was during these mealtimes that our system of "family councils" evolved. I was always encouraged by my parents to bring any issue to the table. For instance, I could discuss everything from whether I could go to Disneyland to whether I should play high school tennis as an eighth-grader. Mom and Dad did not want to be final arbiters in these discussions because they wanted Carl and me to learn how to make decisions by consensus, not by a father stomping his feet or a mother demanding her way. My parents never subscribed to the "it's my way or the highway" theory.

The Chang family liked to take a topic, examine the pros and cons, kick around the benefits and the bad side, and see whether we could come to a conclusion. There was no formal family vote as some have written, but no decision was final until we reached some sort of collective agreement.

Throughout the holiday season in 1987, the issue of the day was what direction my tennis career would take. Obviously, we had been handed a unique situation; players just didn't shoot up from out of nowhere to No. 163 in the world in only six weeks. Then there was my age to consider: I was only fifteen years old and still learning the game.

Two other situations were coloring our decision. Our family had recently moved from La Costa to Placentia, an Orange County suburb. We moved for a couple of reasons: Dad thought I would find better players to practice against in Orange County, and living in Placentia placed us in closer proximity to LAX with its cheaper fares and abundance of flights. Dad had accepted a new position as a research chemist with Unocal, whose offices were located just a handful of blocks from our Placentia home. By staying off the L.A. freeways during commute time, Dad had more time to practice with me after school. I enrolled in nearby Valencia High School for my sophomore year.

As we kicked the topic of turning pro around and around, it became evident that we had four options. They were:

1. *Remain an amateur and maintain the status quo.* At the end of 1987, I was ranked No. 3 in the country for the U.S. Boys 18, behind David Wheaton and Jim Courier, although we felt that the USTA had overlooked me for the top spot. I had won two of the four national tournaments and had beaten Jim at Kalamazoo, which should have bumped me above him. Regarding David Wheaton, traditionally the No. 1 ranking is awarded to the winner of the National 18s, which was me, but David had won the U.S. Open Juniors. This victory caused the USTA to give him the nod. While curious, my family and I did not dwell on it.

The good news was that David and Jim were turning nineteen and would be too old for this age division. That meant I would be the highest-ranked junior left and the favorite to defend my U.S. National title. To improve my tennis, however, I needed to play against players who were *better* than me. That would not happen in junior tennis.

2. *Live at a tennis academy and bang balls from 6 A.M. until 6 P.M.* These days, it seems like every new tennis sensation comes out of a tennis academy, but back when I was weighing whether to turn pro, tennis academies were a fairly recent development. There were only a handful of these boarding academies, all located across the country in the Southeast and Florida. The hot place to go in 1987 was the Nick Bollettieri Tennis Academy in Bradenton, Florida. Run by a former Marine named Nick Bollettieri, dozens of topflight juniors drilled from sunup to sundown. The harsh regimen toughened up their games as boot camp toughened up a barracks full of raw recruits. Our family knew that Andre Agassi had left Las Vegas when he was thirteen for

Bollettieri's, and David Wheaton and Jim Courier were also living and training year-round at Nick's.

Although this appeared to be the direction that junior tennis was heading, tennis academies were never a viable option for me. Mom and Dad didn't feel confident shipping me to the East Coast and into the academy life. They felt it was more important for them to be with me and see me grow up in the kind of loving household they knew they could provide.

Nor was Dad inclined to turn over my game to someone else since he had built my strokes from the ground up. My father also believed that I was one or two years away from challenging any tennis player in the world, and he wanted to guide me through the transition from the juniors to the pros. Besides, tennis academies were expensive—costing tens of thousands of dollars a year—unless I received some sort of scholarship, and those often came with strings attached.

There was another angle to consider. My decision for Christ had sparked a spiritual renewal in my parents. They were becoming acquainted with Proverbs 22:6, which states, "Train a child in the way he should go, and when he is old he will not turn from it." They felt responsible to oversee my physical as well as my spiritual upbringing, and that wasn't going to happen with me boarding in Florida.

And when we came right down to it, we couldn't conceive of being apart during my most formative years. My parents did not want to hand over the responsibility of raising me to someone else. Mom said it best: "Michael, it's like when you don't talk to the Lord each day. You lose contact, you lose communication, and you lose the daily guidance. We don't want that to happen to you."

3. I could go to college and play on a college team. Dad actually came up with this idea after talking with Allen Fox, the tennis coach at

Pepperdine University in Malibu. Coach Fox oversaw a powerhouse program, plus Pepperdine was an hour north off the San Diego Freeway. I would be close to home.

There was the little matter of qualifying *academically* to attend Pepperdine, but Dad thought we had that covered. I had taken my SAT tests in eighth grade and scored over 800, which was good enough to gain entrance. Coach Fox did some checking around in the Pepperdine admissions department and learned that while my case was unusual, the school was ready to accept me.

If I attended Pepperdine, what would that do for my tennis?

I would play top-ranked collegiate players—a significant upgrade in competition from the juniors. But as Dad pointed out, I had played many of the top college players in the satellites, and I had beaten them all.

Then there was the McEnroe model: I could use collegiate tennis as a stepping-stone to the tour. Mac played one year at Stanford, won the NCAA championship in his freshman year, immediately turned pro, and grabbed the tour by the throat as soon as he went out. So did Jimmy Connors, who spent a year at UCLA before turning pro.

The more we thought seriously about the college option, however, the more we realized that it didn't meet our needs. I was fifteen going on sixteen, which meant there was a maturity gap to consider when attending classes and interacting with other college students. My parents weren't ready for me to leave home and be on my own, and I'm not sure if I was mature enough to leave home either. Then we learned that I wouldn't be eligible for the season-ending NCAA tournament (having something to do with eligibility requirements), rendering the issue moot. That news doused water on the entire idea, so we abandoned the college route.

4. *I could turn pro.* Initially, this seemed like the most bodacious

alternative of them all. The pro tour was littered with bodies of young players who had fizzled after a "breakthrough" tournament or season. Whereas girls mature faster and had a history of winning Grand Slam championships as early as age sixteen—such as Maureen Connolly, Tracy Austin, and Martina Hingis—the same was not true in the men's game. Andre Agassi, who had turned pro a year before (in 1986 at the age of sixteen), was struggling on the tour. His breakthrough season would come in 1988, but we didn't know that at the time.

As we considered all four options, I knew I didn't want to play the juniors for another year because I had nothing left to prove. I needed more of a challenge, but turning pro seemed to be quite a leap into the unknown. Swirling around all these thoughts was another factor: Carl had left in the fall for the University of California at Berkeley, which meant I had lost my best practice partner. By now we were used to playing each other for big money—fifty dollars—even though we didn't have the cash! The winner would offer to go double-or-nothing until someone won to bring the bet back to zero. In other words, no one ever had to pay up. I missed our friendly competition.

Dad and I continued our nightly training sessions, and I picked up games at Chapman College with players like Arnaud Deleval, but I missed Carl's presence on the court. Turning pro would also mean waving good-bye to a college scholarship; the NCAA allowed only amateurs to compete in collegiate tennis. "Once a pro, always a pro," was their motto. There would be no backing up on the freeway of professional tennis.

When we celebrated the New Year, we remained uncertain about what 1988 would bring. I knew the decision was weighing on Dad's mind: the expense of sending Mom and me on the road was still in the tens of thousands of dollars annually, except for the pro tournaments that reimbursed us for expenses. Fortunately, Carl was playing at Berkeley on a full scholarship, which helped the family budget, but the pressure to pay for my tennis with after-tax dollars—since my tennis expenses were not tax deductible—was intense.

The thought of turning pro caused a considerable amount of worry. What if I turned pro and started losing first-round matches? What if my ranking fell and I had to fall back into the satellite tournaments? If I turned pro, would my winnings support two people on the road? Mom and Dad knew that they couldn't send a fifteen-year-old boy out on the tour alone. The family agreed that worrying whether I reached a certain round each week (so we could cover our expenses) would put the wrong type of pressure on my young shoulders.

Swirling around us were several prominent tennis agents, all anxious to represent me. We had learned that agents could open doors that we couldn't—such as soliciting wild cards into tournaments or securing clothing and equipment sponsorship contracts. Jeff Austin with Advantage International was one of a handful of agents we had met, and he was obviously courting us. He sized up our situation, and within a month or two, Jeff presented a generous offer from Reebok, a clothing and shoe manufacturer, that he said would solve our immediate cash-flow problems.

Reebok proposed a multiyear deal for a considerable amount of money in exchange for me wearing and promoting Reebok clothes and shoes. This would be more than enough to support Mom and me while I chased ATP points around the world. Worse-case scenario: if I bombed out, there would be money left over to fund college.

In our minds, the Reebok offer sealed the deal. We signed with Jeff to represent us, and then we signed the sponsorship contract with

Reebok. As an added bonus, Jeff secured a wild card into the U.S. Indoors (now known as the Kroger St. Jude) at Memphis in mid-February. I would be making my pro debut while I was still fifteen years old—one week before my sixteenth birthday.

The news that I was turning pro at such a young age was received with skepticism in some quarters. Shortly after Reebok made the announcement, Dad received a letter from Arthur Ashe, head of the ATP Players Council and someone who spoke with great moral authority, based upon his exemplary character. Basically, Arthur told my father that he was crazy to let me turn pro so young—the "stupidest thing possible," he said. Arthur asked us to reconsider.

While we held Arthur in the highest regard, we believed that we had carefully thought through all our options before pulling the pro trigger. But first things first. Before embarking on this new chapter in life, Mom and Dad wanted me to take my GED—a standardized test that showed that I passed high school. They didn't want me to be tagged as a "high school dropout" each time I played a tournament. I passed my GED with flying colors four days after getting my wisdom teeth pulled. In the middle of my sophomore year, I was officially a puffy-cheeked high school graduate.

GOING DOWN TO MEMPHIS

I'll never forget arriving at the Racquet Club of Memphis and being greeted by Tommy Buford, the tournament director.

"Howya doin', Michael?" he said, pumping my arm. "We're sure glad to have you here. We got you all set up. If you ever need anything, just let us know."

Tommy, I learned subsequently, says that *every* year. He is one of the good guys in tennis, and he is the reason I have returned to Memphis every February since 1988. Tommy informed me that my first match as a professional would be against Ricky Leach, a lefty from Southern California. I knew the Leach name because I had grown up playing his younger brother, right-handed Jonathan, in the juniors. Ricky, known more as a doubles specialist, possessed a wicked left-handed serve.

I never thought twice about competing against someone older and more experienced; I had been doing it since I was six years old. I even played in *men's* divisions while I was still in elementary school. When I was twelve years old, Dad entered me in a Men's B tournament in nearby Fallbrook, which I won handily. "Next year, we'll move you up to the Men's Open," he said afterward. I thought that was a bit much, but a year later I captured the Men's Open.

I beat Ricky in straight sets in my pro debut, but then I came up against Ramesh Krishnan, a twenty-six-year-old Indian player who sliced and diced his shots on the fast indoor courts. Ramesh wasn't any taller than I was, so for once, I was playing against someone of equal stature. We soon found ourselves in a long, three-set struggle. Then I began experiencing cramps in my calves—and my arms! This was the first time that painful cramps pulsated through my body, and I panicked a bit on the court. As I slowed down, Ramesh picked up his game and closed out the match.

Afterward, my body got worse. My chest began cramping in the locker room, and then my entire body was fighting the painful spasms. I moaned in agony.

"Am I dying?" I asked Todd Snyder, the ATP trainer, as only an inexperienced fifteen-year-old could.

"You'll make it, Chief," he said.

Jeff Austin, my agent, was called to the trainer's room, and he immediately became frightened by what he saw—the sight of me hyperventilating as I struggled with exhaustion. It was a scary situation since it was the first time I had to deal with serious cramping.

Cramps became such a worry in those early years that I made it a practice to drink water by the gallons—or so it seemed—following each match. During my first summer on tour, I played an exhibition tournament in North Carolina. After an intense singles match, I forced myself to quaff glass after glass of cool, refreshing water to ward off cramps. I had an incentive to drink so much: following my break, I was supposed to play a doubles match to round off the event. I didn't want cramps to cramp my doubles.

A big crowd was on hand as the match began. My partner and I took a 5–4 lead late in the first set. As we sat down during the changeover, all the water I had gulped an hour before was sending a loud-and-clear signal that nature was calling. I pondered whether to take a bathroom break. *Nah. It can wait until the set is over,* I thought.

The strong urge to go to the bathroom did not abate when we resumed play. My partner was serving for the set, but we couldn't quite pocket the set. The game went to deuce. Deuce a second time. A third, fourth, and fifth time. My bladder was ready to explode!

With the score still at deuce, I dropped my racket and sprinted for the bathroom. Of course, all five thousand people knew *exactly* where I was going since they could see me heading for the stadium restroom. When I returned I was greeted by a rousing ovation—and lots of laughter.

Another rookie year incident wasn't so funny. One time a big-name pro agreed to practice with me. After warming up our groundies, he came to the net and practiced his volley for about five minutes. When he was done, I moved up to the net while he returned to the baseline and hit ground strokes to me.

In those days, however, my volleys weren't very good. Anxious to please this famous player, I either underhit or overhit: either my volleys landed in the net or I poked them long and out of reach. I couldn't hit a volley back into the court if my life depended upon it.

Brian Gottfried, a former touring player who had become a USTA coach, was giving me some pointers at the time. Brian stood by the court, watching me struggle to hit two clean volleys consecutively. Finally, the big-name pro had had enough.

He walked to the side of the court and got a drink of water.

"Tell you what, Brian," he said after he took a long sip. "Why don't you warm up Michael's volleys and overheads, and we'll pick it up from there when you're done."

Most of the time life on the tour was not as awkward, thanks to Mom, although I'm sure the two of us were an unusual sight. She traveled with me everywhere, on a circuit where you don't see mothers and sons too often. The reason you don't see many moms is that most male tennis pros aren't good enough to play with the big boys until they are nineteen, twenty, twenty-one years old—an age when they are supposedly mature enough to travel without a mother in tow.

My situation was completely different, of course. I *had* to have a parental or guardian-like chaperone on the tour; it would have been some form of child abuse to let me go out on my own at age sixteen. Also, my parents did not want me to face the adult world of pro tennis alone. Mom and Dad were concerned about the unhealthy lifestyles of star athletes in the limelight, the dangers of peer pressure, and the enormous temptations afforded

by fame and money. They wanted to shield me from these potential pit-
falls. Looking back, I'm glad that they did the right thing.

Having Mom around didn't become a problem with other players
because she was so personable. Nobody ever asked, "What's she doing
out here?" Instead, they responded by saying, "Oh, that's Mrs. Chang.
She's cool."

Mom could get along with anybody because of her winning personality. She had a way of making friends, and I can remember more than
a few players telling their life stories while Mom listened and offered
tea and sympathy. She was great to have around for other reasons as
well. One, she could cook for me, which kept me eating healthy meals
before my matches. She also handled our travel arrangements, screened
my phone calls, and sewed my shorts. She kept track of details great
and small—even stenciling the P on the strings of my Prince racket.
All this allowed me to concentrate on my tennis. Finally, if I had no
practice partner, Mom wasn't bashful about approaching another
player and inquiring whether he could hit with me. I was too timid to
ask someone I had watched play on TV. Not Mom. She was never too
shy to ask—thank goodness!

You could tell that she cared about the other players too. I remember the time when Pete Sampras asked her whether she had anything
to help him get over a bad case of diarrhea. It turns out she did have
something. Mom spread a little motherly love on a cutthroat tour
where the only time you heard the word *love* was when the umpire
announced a score.

There's another funny story that I have to tell, which shows what
naive rookies we were when we started traveling together. A month
after playing Memphis, we flew to Miami for the Lipton tournament.

At the player's hotel, we strolled up to the concierge and asked him to recommend a good restaurant.

"What type of food are you interested in?" asked the concierge.

"Seafood," Mom replied. "We want to have some seafood since Florida is right on the coast." I knew that Mom loved crab, corn, and fresh bread. That was her favorite restaurant meal.

The concierge mulled that request for a moment before saying, "There's a shopping area right next to the hotel. Go outside and take a left, and you'll see the restaurant. They have good seafood."

The concierge was right. We walked five minutes and found the restaurant with no problem. The place looked busy, but we took that to be a good sign. Within minutes, we were seated and handed menus. A few minutes later, our waitress dropped by our table. My eyes popped out. She was wearing a white T-shirt that appeared to be eight sizes too small, leaving open a bare midriff. Completing her outfit were orange hot pants, pantyhose, and white sneakers.

"Can I get you anything from the bar?" she asked in a perky voice.

We shook our heads and turned back to our menus. Mom and I started with raw oysters as an appetizer, and then she ordered her favorite meal—crab and corn. Meanwhile, I ordered some steamers and fish.

While we waited for our food, we noticed the other waitresses walking by, each carrying their orders to hungry customers. All were wearing the same outfit—tight T-shirts and orange hot pants. I noticed that they all had great figures.

"That one is pretty," said Mom.

"Yes, that one is pretty," I agreed.

"Have you noticed what the waitresses are wearing?" Mom asked as we shared the oyster appetizer.

"Uh, it's hard not to notice."

"Well, those outfits are a little revealing," she commented.

When our meals arrived, we dug in. "The food is very good here," said Mom as she broke open a crab claw.

"Sure is, Mom."

"What's the name of this restaurant?" she asked.

"I think it's called Hooters."

"Hooters? Never heard of it," she said.

"Neither have I."

A few nights later, we returned to Hooters for another evening of good seafood. We had found our spot in Miami—a Hooters restaurant.

Two years passed, and I was talking with some of the guys in the Lipton locker room when the topic of restaurants came up. I mentioned that I knew the name of a really good seafood restaurant in the area.

"Really, what's the name?" asked one pro. Everyone on the tour likes to know about a good restaurant.

"It's called Hooters."

"You took your mother to Hooters?" exclaimed one pro. The locker room filled with laughter.

"What's wrong with Hooters?" I asked.

That set off another round of laughter. The next day, some of the guys teased. "Hey, Mrs. Chang, we heard Michael took you to Hooters!"

In the months to come, I felt accepted where it counted most—the locker room. While some of the older players liked teasing me, most of the guys on the tour were helpful. Three that stand out were the doubles team of Ken Flach and Robert Seguso and a South African player named Johan Kriek—veterans who were ten to twelve years older than me. We didn't become best buds, but they were always nice to Mom and me.

OUR FIRST VISIT TO PARIS

I had a good spring, which launched me into the top 100 and meant I didn't have to qualify to play in Grand Slam events. First up was the French Open, and Mom and I were awed by Paris and Roland Garros, just as we expected we would be. I had always dreamed of getting here, but the thought of serving on the red clay with the Eiffel Tower not far away . . . I got goose bumps just thinking about it.

When the draw came out, I did some "charting," as the players call it. If I won my first two matches and John McEnroe won *his* first two matches, we had a date at Roland Garros. Now that is what I call incentive.

I had been "beating" John ever since I took him on in the basement of our Minnesota home. He was the guy who I enjoyed watching compete at Wimbledon when I was in the second grade—and the famous player that I always came from behind to beat in Nerf tennis after losing the first two sets. Of course, that was a seven-year-old boy's imagination working overtime.

We each won our first two matches, and suddenly people were talking about this "interesting matchup" between a sixteen-year-old teen who grew up dreaming that he beat McEnroe in a Grand Slam tournament versus the controversial twenty-nine-year-old Mighty Mac, winner of seven Grand Slams.

When the press asked John to size up the match, he said, "I'm going to teach this kid what it's like to play on the tour." He wasn't smiling when he said it. John was determined that my first big-name match would be a tennis lesson, and I would have to pay for it at the door.

I'll never forget what happened when we walked out on Court 1— the last match of the day. Anticipation had been building for hours;

there wasn't an empty seat in the stands or in the walkways. John scooted in front of me so he could walk out onto the court first, and I practically curtsied to let him pass by.

Big mistake. He led us onto Court 1, and the French crowd—which loves expressive people and had always taken a liking to John—gave him a tumultuous roar. John raised both arms up to acknowledge the fans, who responded by going even more nuts. Walking ten steps behind, I felt like a schoolboy who should be carrying his racket bag.

John rushed me from the get-go. He won the first nine points of the match, then finished the first set in twenty-four minutes, 6–0. He ran me ragged in the second set to win 6–1. I started fighting back in the third after the intimidation factor had worn off, but John had more than enough game left to win the third and final set 6–3. A master pro *had* given me a tennis lesson.

In summation, I'll say this: playing John proved to be an invaluable experience, and I used that knowledge a year later at the 1989 French Open.

HELLO, AMERICA!

Several other things happened in 1988 that are worth noting. The first occurred at the U.S. Open, where I had a great tournament and was introduced into America's living rooms.

I won my first two rounds, which placed me in a weekend match against "Dr. Dirt," a scrappy player named Tim Wilkison. Back in those days, live televised broadcasts were limited to weekend coverage on the CBS network (wall-to-wall coverage on the USA network started a couple of years later). The CBS cameras were poised on our match when we were hit by a sudden thunderstorm at 3–2 in the fifth set. Tim and I ran for the locker room to wait out the rain delay. When we came out an hour later, I squeaked out a close match, 6–4 in the fifth. CBS Sports wanted an on-court interview with me immediately following the match.

"How were you able to stay so calm during the rain delay?" asked Andrea Joyce, the CBS reporter on the scene.

"Because of the Lord Jesus Christ," I answered.

She was so stunned that she didn't know what to say. End of interview.

"Back up to you, Brent," she said, "tossing" the broadcast back to Brent Musberger, who was leading the CBS coverage at the time.

Three weeks later in San Francisco, I was practicing in the old Cow Palace for the Transamerica Open tournament. Our one-hour hitting session was called "four on a court" because four players had to share a single court in the indoor arena. I was hitting away from the baseline when I looked to the other side of the net and noticed that my hitting partner appeared blurry.

I had never noticed that before. I rubbed my eyes to be sure. My hitting partner was still fuzzy-looking. I said to the person hitting next to me, "I know this is a strange question, but when you look to the other side of the court, is it blurry?"

"No," he replied. "Why do you ask?"

"I think something is not right with my eyes."

I went to the eye doctor the next day—he was the father of a friend of Carl's in Berkeley—and sure enough, I needed correction in both eyes. Not much, since I was .125 in both eyes, but enough to matter, said the optometrist. I was given a prescription for contact lenses.

Later that day, with my eyeballs wearing fresh contact lenses, I went out to hit some more balls. The experience was eye-opening, all right: I could see everything, especially the intricate spin on the fuzzy yellow ball. The tennis ball looked as big as a basketball—that's how well I was seeing it.

I played great at the Transamerica—so well, in fact, that I won my first professional tournament. I was not, however, the youngest ever to accomplish that feat; that distinction belonged to Aaron Krickstein, who was five months younger when he won a tournament in Tel Aviv in 1983. I defeated Johan Kriek in the finals, and he had kind words for me at the trophy presentation. "What we have here is a young kid who is not only a great player but humble, and we need more people like him on the tour," said Johan.

When I heard those remarks, I shuffled my feet and looked down, embarrassed that he was saying such nice things about me. Nonetheless, I appreciated him making that statement.

A week after the Transamerica, something happened to top my first pro title: I was baptized at my grandparents' church in Thousand Oaks on October 23. I know, because I have the date inscribed in the palm-sized Bible I often travel with.

I had wanted to get baptized during the summer, but there hadn't been time with my hectic tennis schedule. Besides, the pastor of Gohng-Gohng's church wanted to sit down with me for a friendly interview before he would baptize me. We weren't able to get together until after the Transamerica, however. When we did sit down face-to-face, the interview came off as awkward.

With my grandfather also in attendance, the pastor began talking to me about giving money to the church and what that involved. I squirmed uncomfortably in my chair. I had been expecting the pastor to explain what baptism was all about or pepper me with questions like, "How do you know you're a Christian?" or "What does your faith mean to you?"

Instead, I felt like I was being hit up for money. As I've matured in my faith, I've learned that "each man should give what he has decided in his heart to give, not reluctantly or under compulsion, for God loves a cheerful giver," as Paul says in 2 Corinthians 9:7. At age sixteen and a baby Christian, I could not be expected to understand the biblical concept of giving as I do today.

I was baptized during the Sunday morning church service with several other young people. The Chinese Christian Church had a baptismal tub in the front: I remember standing in a white gown (with shorts and shirt on underneath), waiting to get dunked. When the pastor asked me if I believed that Jesus Christ had died for my sins and if I wished to be baptized, I nodded yes. Then the pastor held me as he leaned me back into the water. When I bounced back up, I thanked and praised the Lord for His goodness.

All in all, 1988 was a very good year: I got baptized in the church *and* on the professional tennis tour. Yet looking back, I realize how incredible God's timing was. I am fortunate that I became a Christian *before* I turned pro and *before* I won the French Open a year later. I don't think I would have handled everything that came my way after Paris very well without the Lord's guidance. While winning Roland Garros was definitely a blessing, in many ways it turned out to be an experience of growth and maturity because of the many added expectations.

Courtesy of Curtis Chew

• GOLFING WITH CARL AT WHISTLER •

CHAPTER 7

SOME BROTHERLY COACHING

Expectations are a funny thing. Mine went through the roof after I won the French Open in 1989. It's not that I *expected* many more Grand Slam titles in my future, but the thought certainly crossed my mind that I had many years left to win a *few* more. I know that Jim Courier, Andre Agassi, and Pete Sampras believed they could win a Grand Slam after witnessing a fellow traveler in the U.S. junior universe perform the same trick. They formed a line to see who could be next. (It turned out to be Pete at the 1990 U.S. Open when he became the youngest male to win a U.S. Open at age nineteen.)

Of course, that's what makes competition great—you never know what's going to happen. The *unexpected* happened to me a couple of weeks before Christmas in 1989. I was practicing in Florida when I sprinted for a backhand deep in the corner. As I stretched for the ball, I heard a loud crack—in my hip! I fell down as if I had been shot. When I picked myself up, it was all I could do to limp off the court under my own power.

Dr. Paul Shirley, the ATP's medical director, examined me at the Baptist Medical Center in Jacksonville, Florida. X-rays determined that I had fractured the cup of the left hip joint at the point where the ball goes into the socket. The freakish injury mystified medical experts because they were used to seeing these types of fractures in seventy-year-old men, not seventeen-year-old teenagers. Back in Los Angeles, Dr. Robert Kerlan, a noted sports physician, informed me that I had really done a number on my hip. He showed me the X-ray, which revealed a small crack about two millimeters wide in my hip socket.

All sorts of scenarios raced through my mind as I scanned the X-ray. I reminded myself to remain calm since God was still in control. He knew about the hip fracture, and He knew what my future held. Still, the news hit me hard, especially in terms of my emotions. I imagined all sorts of terrible things happening—like the hip not healing properly or that I would lose a step. My game was built around speed, and if I couldn't scoot around the court, I would be the youngest male *never* to defend a Grand Slam title.

Dr. Kerlan, while sober about the severity of the injury, remained optimistic that my hip fracture required neither surgery nor a cast—just some good rest. He believed that I did not suffer a fracture, but instead experienced a separation of the bone in the area of my left hip socket. He handed me a pair of crutches and told me to hobble around on those for a month or so. "It's important to keep weight off that hip of yours," he instructed.

The Chang family experienced a quiet Christmas. After four weeks on crutches, I began spending time in the gym to get back into shape. I was told not to exercise the hip area, however, but to continue to rest it. When I felt ready to hit balls, I gingerly stepped on the practice court. Within a week or two I felt close to normal, but I postponed my 1990 tour debut to late February at the U.S. Indoors in Memphis. Director Tommy Buford didn't quite put a bear hug on me when I returned to play in his indoor tournament, but he was certainly happy to see me.

The feeling was mutual. I didn't hang around long, however, as Glenn Layendecker decked me in the first round. We wondered if I had come back too soon. Another thing we noticed was that my hip was fine for the first couple of hours of playing, but then it got sore in the third hour and my performance dropped rapidly. We found that puzzling. It was then that I hired a trainer, Ken Matsuda, to rehabilitate my hip and improve my movement. (I continue to work with Ken to this day.)

Throughout the spring, I could feel the tension building. The French Open was coming up, and people were wondering if this Chang kid was capable of defending his title. Meanwhile, my mind was playing the expectations game and worrying whether my hip would come around 100 percent. It didn't help my confidence when I didn't win a match in three clay court tournaments leading up to the French Open. On top of that, I played a couple of exhibition matches and lost both. One was a close three-setter to Andres Gomez that I gave away after blowing a 4–1 lead in the final set. Mentally, I had lost it on the court, and after the match, I lost it emotionally when tears started streaming down. I never felt so low in my young life.

The press certainly noticed the springtime slump. I received such questions as, "Where's your God now?" and "Do you still credit Jesus Christ when you lose?" The sharp knives were out.

On the Sunday before the start of the French Open, the tournament invited a couple of dozen players to play for charity at Roland Garros. Playing these benefit matches before a large, friendly crowd at Court Central was a good way to get a feel for the court and ease your way into the tournament. The players kick back and try to have some fun before playing for keeps.

The format called for the players to play a pro-set—first one to eight games wins. I was asked to play Jean-Phillippe Fleurian, a popular French player. Since I had not won a match on clay all spring, I had my game face on. I needed to beat Jean-Phillipe and build my confidence.

When Jean-Phillipe noticed that I was playing hard, he wiped his "Hi, glad to be here" grin off his face and began engaging me in the duel. Before long, we had dialed up the intensity level to something on the order of say, the fifth set of the French Open final. When I hit a good shot, I pumped my fists like I did against Stefan Edberg a year earlier. When Jean-Phillipe ripped a winner, he reacted strongly as well. Let's just say that there was a whole lot of fist pumping going on for an exhibition match.

People started laughing because it was so ridiculous, but I needed to win a match—even a pro-set for charity! When I conquered Jean-Phillipe 8–7, I was pretty pleased and pumped at the same time. I can't remember if the capacity crowd at Court Central clapped, whistled, or hee-hawed, but at least I can chuckle about it now.

I did not have a cheery defense of my French Open crown, but I did win four matches and reach the quarterfinals before losing to Andre Agassi in four sets. Andre advanced to his first French final, where he met the thirty-year-old Ecuadorian, Andres Gomez. Andres, fresh off an exhibition win against me, outplayed Andre to capture his late-in-life first Grand Slam.

TRANSITION TIME

My tennis career following the 1989 French Open up through 1991 felt like it was two steps forward and one step back. My ranking yo-yoed from No. 5 to 24 to 10 to the middle teens—and languished there. I won only two tournaments, and I could never put together a consistent stretch during a two-week Grand Slam tournament.

My father believed that my serve was the chink in my armor. When I won the French Open, my serves averaged 77 mph and topped out at 89 mph. (Don't laugh. The racket technology has greatly improved since that time.) By contrast, Stefan Edberg was a good 20 mph faster than I that day: he averaged 97 and topped out at 109. We had thought that as my body matured and I could start lifting weights (we were counseled not to start weight training until I was nineteen or so), my beefed-up body would start blasting aces whenever I needed a big point.

We hired Phil Dent to help with my serve. Phil, an Aussie, was a former touring pro and lived in the Newport Beach area, not far from Placentia, so it made sense to bring Phil on board and see if he could help me.

Meanwhile, Carl was finishing up his senior year at Berkeley in the spring of 1991. During school breaks, Carl came out on tour with Mom and me every chance he could, and it was fun to practice with my old hitting partner.

We even played a couple of doubles tournaments together while Carl was still in college. I'll never forget our first doubles match in the pros. Carl and I had received a wild card into the Washington, D.C., event held every July. Bad draw: our first-round match would be against Richey Reneberg and Jim Grabb, who were, at the time, the best U.S. doubles team and the tournament's top seed.

We were scheduled to play the second match of the evening session, and the outdoor stadium was packed with at least five thousand people. I noticed that Carl was pretty nervous before we left the locker room. When we walked onto the court, Carl had that wide-eyed, "deer in the headlights" look.

"We're going to do just fine," I said.

"Go ahead, you serve first," gulped Carl. I couldn't blame my older brother for being a bit uptight. This was his first professional match, and a big nighttime crowd was on hand to watch us play.

I served the first point of the match to Jim Grabb in the deuce court. My strong spin serve took Jim out wide, so he flicked up a short lob toward Carl—a super sitter. Carl turned his shoulders to smash an overhead and deliver the coup de grâce. He swung as hard as he could and struck the ball at the very top of the frame, which caused the ball to shoot almost straight up in the air—like a jump ball!

Jim and Richey, of course, had backed up all the way to the fence because they expected Carl to bludgeon the ball into the rear grandstand. Instead, all four of us watched Carl's crazy-eight rim shot come down to earth barely on their side of the net and then spin back over the net on to *our* side. Under the rules, we were not obliged to hit the ball back. Point to the Chang brothers!

The crowd went nuts, Carl took a bow, and we went on to lose a well-played match in straight sets. But we had a great time.

Later that summer, we paired up again at New Haven, Connecticut. The tournament put us on center court again with a big crowd, but this time Carl and I put it together and won our first-round match. Carl's first pro victory vaulted him to the top 400 in the world in doubles, and my brother sported an ear-to-ear grin until he had to return to school in the fall.

I don't know how Carl juggled tennis and classwork while he attended Cal. He was a fine collegiate player who graduated on time in June 1991 with a degree in international business. He specialized in classes on the political economy of industrialized society, business administration, and economics. I'm proud that he excelled in the classroom while tackling tough courses.

Carl, like most college graduates, wasn't sure what he wanted to do with his life. He thought about it some, then decided that since he was footloose and free, he wanted to try playing on the tour. The reality for Carl is that when you don't have a world ranking, or if your world ranking has three digits in it rather than two, you're relegated to the minor leagues of the sport—the "Challenger" and Satellite events.

The Challengers and Satellites are the equivalent of rookie ball: these entry-level circuits can be found in Asia, South America, Europe, and the United States. Hundreds of young players travel the globe in search of elusive ATP points in tournaments with total purses of twenty-five thousand dollars, more or less. First-round losers take home a few hundred bucks.

Challengers were light-years away from my world—glitzy million-dollar tournaments held at fancy resorts with corporate sponsor tents and hundreds of volunteers available for our every need. For instance, when the top pros arrive a few days before the tournament, we can show up at the site and ask for just about anything.

Player transportation?

We have Mercedes courtesy cars this week, Mr. Chang. Which color would you like?

I'm a bit hungry.

We have brought in three chefs from Paris this week who are waiting to prepare anything you want . . .

Practice courts?

No problem, Mr. Chang. When would you like to play?

Practice balls?

Here are a couple of cans, Mr. Chang. Would you like more?

Towels?

Mr. Chang, take as many as you want.

Do you have something to drink?

What can we get for you, Mr. Chang? We have Gatorade, bottled water, Coke, other sports drinks . . .

You get the idea. Now, I've never been one to try to take advantage of the volunteers at the tournament desk. I have never wanted people to bow and scrape to me because I believe in the Golden Rule: "Do to others as you would have them do to you," says Luke 6:31. I've sought to treat others as I would hope to be treated by them if I were in their position.

After graduation, Carl came out on tour with me for a few weeks as he considered his options for the future. Then, he decided to try his hand at becoming a professional tennis player himself. This was certainly the time in his life to give it a shot. He searched around and found a Challenger event in Singapore. After I finished playing the U.S. Open in 1991, Dad and Carl hopped on a long flight and arrived in hot and sticky Singapore. At the player's hotel, they learned that nobody played or practiced until four in the afternoon.

The next day, Carl sauntered out to the tennis grounds to find someone to hit a few balls with. He rounded up another player and then approached the tournament desk. Since Carl had accompanied me to a couple dozen tournaments, he was used to a certain level of service. Like someone ordering at a fast-food drive-through window,

Carl asked for some court time, a couple of cans of balls, two towels, cold water . . .

The Singapore tennis official behind the modest table was suitably unimpressed. "This is Challenger," he said. "Not the U.S. Open."

The Singapore man reached into a box of old balls and handed Carl two fuzzless versions. "If you want better practice balls next time, you'll have to return these when you're done," he said. "Here are your towels," he said, holding up another box to Carl. He peered inside and saw a boxful of towels that looked like they had last been washed when Ronald Reagan was president.

Carl lost in the first round of singles, but he played doubles with Greg Rusedski and reached the semifinals. Dad and Carl flew back home, and during that long trip home, they began talking.

"What would you think of coaching Michael?" Dad asked.

The possibility stunned Carl.

"Why me?"

"I think Michael needs a change, plus he needs a full-time coach who can travel everywhere with him. Phil Dent can't do that since he has a young family. Besides, there is no one who knows his game as well as you do."

Dad did have a point. Carl knew my game inside and out since he had spent thousands of hours on the same court with me. He was a knowledgeable player who had always been a thinker on the court—such as the time he suggested I adjust my eyes from the summer sun by going indoors early before my big match with Al Parker. He could pick out players' weaknesses like an ice skating judge appraising a long-program performance.

I remember one such time in 1990, when Carl was beginning his senior year at Berkeley and I was playing Davis Cup for the United States against Austria. The match was held in Vienna in cold and cool conditions for late September. No one was predicting that we would waltz through the Austrian team since they were playing before seventeen thousand rabid Austrian fans in a soccer stadium converted into a tennis venue. The Austrians painted their faces in red to match the Austrian flag and chanted *Zugabe! Zugabe!* ("Do it again! Do it again!") in decibels rivaling a World Cup *fussball* match. Austria had never reached the Davis Cup semifinals before, and with Thomas Muster and Horst Skoff playing on their favorite surface—red clay—they felt that the overconfident Americans were ripe for the taking.

I didn't feel overconfident, mainly because I was still in the midst of a slump following my debilitating hip injury. We did have Andre Agassi on the team, but Andre had lost in the finals of the French and U.S. Open that year, and people were speculating that he would never win the big one. (Andre wouldn't win his first Grand Slam, at Wimbledon, for another two years.)

Thomas beat me in four sets in the opening rubber, but Andre came back and demolished Horst Skoff. Our doubles team of Rick Leach and Jim Pugh cruised through the doubles, and the tie looked to be ours when Andre squared off against Muster. Feeding off Andre's pace and the roaring of the crowd, however, Muster easily handled Andre in straight sets.

That set the stage for the fifth and final match that would decide the U.S.-Austria tie—Chang versus Skoff. Little did I know that it would take twenty-five hours to complete this exciting and memorable match.

Horst Skoff played like Ronald Agenor—all forehand and a chip backhand. His best surface was clay because the slow surface gave him time to run around his backhand and whale on his forehand. When we squared off on Sunday afternoon, the Austrian fans were determined to lift their hero to victory over the American—me.

Horst jumped out in front and won the first two sets, and now it was do or die. I knew I could come back: Ever since I had lost to Nduko Odizor in five sets in my U.S. Open debut in 1987, I had won seven straight five-set matches. But winning three straight sets appeared insurmountable before a hostile audience who clapped for every error from me and roared each time Horst hit a winner.

It was starting to get dark when we started the third set; there was no way we could complete a five-set match at Prater Stadium—which had no lights—before darkness. *Just win the third set,* I told myself. *Then you can regroup overnight and come back tomorrow.*

I broke early in the third set and held on, so the umpire had no option but to suspend the match into Monday. Dad had joined Mom and me in Austria, and after the match, Dad suggested that I call Carl in California and glean any advice from him.

It was still Sunday morning in Berkeley when I reached Carl by phone. He had no clue what had transpired in Vienna, so I brought him up to date.

"What do you think?" I asked.

Carl thought for a moment. "Isn't ESPN televising the match tonight?"

I didn't know, but Carl quickly confirmed that ESPN was tape-delaying the match and showing it Sunday night in the U.S.

"Tell you what," said Carl. "I'll watch the match later tonight, and then I'll call you in the morning, your time."

Carl stayed up until eleven o'clock Sunday evening watching me play the first three sets against Horst. Then he called my hotel room, where local time was 8 A.M. Monday in Austria. I had barely slept because I was so worried about the outcome. The entire Davis Cup tie was riding on my shoulders.

"Obviously, Skoff is running around his forehand every time," Carl noted. "This is what you have to do. You have to get him to hit his backhand, so don't hit your regular cross-court backhand. He just runs around that and smacks his forehand. You have to hit a slow, angle backhand that takes him so far off the court that he has to hit his backhand. When he does that, hit the next shot to his forehand. He'll run across the court to hit his forehand, but now he's leaving his whole backhand side open. Hit it there and make him hit another backhand. Now you're taking his favorite shot away from him. He's not going to play as well when he has to hit more backhands. Then the whole court will open up."

"Thanks, Carl. I'll give it a try."

"You can also move way over to the alley when you serve from the ad court," he continued. "Then kick your serve to his backhand. He doesn't like to hit that shot."

Our match was delayed that morning because of rain, which made the court slower and the balls heavier. Carl's tactics worked like a charm, and I stormed back to take the fourth set. In the fifth and deciding set, I continued to use the kick serve to Horst's backhand with success, but I also resurrected the Lendl Position and crept up close to the service line to return serve. The tactic worked: although Horst didn't double-fault, he did serve some fat serves that I knocked away for winners.

I felt in control when I took a 5–3 lead in the fifth set—but then my legs started cramping. Not again!

These cramps in my quads were as painful as anything I had

experienced. I wasn't exhausted. Nervous tension and my inability to stay loose playing in gloomy weather with temperatures in the low fifties caused the cramps. Two points from the match, my legs locked up, and I seriously wondered if I had one more game left in me.

I reached match point at 15–40 on Horst's serve, and when he spun one in, I took a full swing and smacked a cross-court winner off my forehand. And all I heard was quiet. The Austrian crowd, in full-throated roar just minutes earlier, stood up and filed out of the stadium. It was kind of like an NFL kicker winning a road game on a long field goal in the final seconds. Total silence.

Carl's advice had been the difference for my biggest Davis Cup victory. Now I needed his help to turn around my career. At another one of our family-council meetings, Mom, Dad, Carl, and I weighed the pros and cons like we normally did when a big decision faced the family.

"I think I can help you," said Carl with a conviction that surprised even me. "I know your strengths and your weaknesses. I've played against Jim, Pete, and Andre. I know their games as well. But most of all, I have a vision for your game. I want to build on your strengths and turn your weaknesses into strengths. Your strengths are your ground strokes, mental toughness, and foot speed. I would like to keep those as a foundation and make you more of an all-court player."

"Good," I said. "Let's get started."

COACH CARL

News that my older brother was going to coach me was greeted with some raised eyebrows and probably provoked a few smirks in the tennis world. *What does he know?* they said. *Carl's never played on the tour.*

He bombed out on the Challenger circuit. Michael is just looking for a traveling companion—his brother.

Those whispers couldn't be farther from the truth, and as history has shown, Carl took my game to the next level. When you look at my career record, my best years stretched from 1992 to 1997, when I cracked the top 10 and stayed there. I came within one match of becoming the No. 1 player in the world. Carl helped my game in small ways and in huge leaps.

There was another benefit when Carl became my full-time coach. Mom could finally take a break from all the travel and spend more time with Dad. Nobody ever saw what a huge sacrifice—more than four years of her life—that Mom had made to travel with me from Miami to Malaysia. Everyone except those who travel for a living thinks the road life is glamorous, but it's not. The time away from home for Mom meant time away from Dad, and I could tell how much they missed each other upon her return. Dad would go out of his way to be nice to Mom after he picked us up at LAX. He would say things that I didn't normally hear him say: how much he missed her, how much he missed her good cooking, and how much he missed not having her to talk to. They would take walks around the neighborhood and hold hands.

Besides being extra nice, Dad honored Mom by making sure the house was extra clean because Mom was such an immaculate person. He made sure everything was picked up and that her plants were watered. Those were big things to Mom.

Now we were about to enter a new phase: Team Chang. We had always been a close-knit group, but now our roles were becoming more clearly defined. It reminded me of what I had been reading in the *Student Bible* about how we are all parts of one body—the body of Christ. First Corinthians 12:12 says, "The body is a unit, though it is made up of many parts; and though all its parts are many, they form one body. So it is with Christ."

The apostle Paul, the author of that passage, was comparing the body of Christ to the human body. Each part has a specific function that is necessary to the body as a whole. The parts are different for a purpose, and their differences must work together. Paul further explained that as members of God's family, we may have different functions and gifts, but we have a common goal. In our case, God had blessed us with my tennis career; Carl and I would work together toward that common goal.

Dad retired from his job with Unocal to manage my financial affairs, and this took a big load off my shoulders. Again, the public never sees how much behind-the-scenes work is needed to keep a tennis career organized and track all the contracts, prize money, and accounts payable and receivable. During my best stretch, I could have worked 365 days a year on some tennis-related endeavor: a tournament, an exhibition, an appearance, a clinic, or an interview. I needed balance, and Carl, Mom, and Dad were able to provide that for me.

When Carl became my coach and traveling companion, Mom was freed up to assist Dad with the workload and help out where she saw a need. From the outset, we were determined to maintain *perspective*. To the Chang family, tennis was a means to an end, and that end was for me to influence people's lives for the good.

First, Carl had to improve my serve. It didn't take a rocket scientist—or a chemist like my dad—to see how the game had accelerated since I won the French Open. A technological breakthrough in racket construction had turned tennis into a power game. A new wave of bigger, taller players was coming on tour: Richard Krajicek, Sergi Bruguera, Michael Stich, and Goran Ivanisevic, to name a few. (These days, about seventeen out of the top twenty players are six feet tall or more.) Against these big hitters, I was having to work hard to earn points on my serve because my opponents were taking my relatively weaker offerings and blasting them back, immediately putting me on the defensive. I needed a serve that would give me one or two free points a game.

Another issue was at hand. Because I was working so hard to win my serve, I had to work hard to win matches. I needed to cut down on marathon five-setters in the Slams because they were wearing me out for the later rounds.

When Carl initially "suggested" some improvements in my serve, however, it took me a while to come around. I am stubborn by nature; but then Carl tactfully pointed out that I had been stuck in the mid-teens in the world rankings and had not come close to winning another Grand Slam since Paris in 1989.

"I'm not talking about changing you into a serve-and-volleyer," said Carl. "I'm talking about upping your first-serve percentage and looking at ways we can increase your speed so we can get some free points."

We started with my ball toss on the serve. "We need a higher toss, but one that is out more to the right," said Carl. "It's like a pitcher throwing to home plate. He doesn't release the ball from over his head. No, he releases the ball right here at one o'clock," said Carl as he pointed with his racket to a point on the face of an imaginary clock. "That's his power zone, and it's going to be yours as well."

Carl watched me serve some more. "Obviously, you're not blessed with height, but you're blessed with strong legs," he said. "You need to push off with your legs as much as you can—and jump into the court."

Carl worked long hours with me. He suggested putting my feet farther apart, coiling more with my torso, and making sure my elbow was making a strong right angle. He called this the "power snap position." My serve didn't improve by leaps and bounds overnight, but I made slow and steady progress, which is the best kind. Within a year, my serve had improved tremendously, and I was falling into the court, ready to pounce on a short ball. This development made me much more aggressive mentally each time I stepped up to the baseline, but it was another innovation from Carl that turned my formerly defensive serve into an offensive weapon.

THE LONG AND SHORT OF IT

Carl was quite a student of the game—a fast learner who adapted to the tour life quickly. Once he learned something, he never had to ask about it again. He took care of everything: what time to warm up; what time to eat before a match; stringing up my rackets before my matches; knowing how many rackets were strung at a certain tension (Carl became an expert stringer. In a pinch, he could string up one of my frames in under fifteen minutes.); having clean Reebok clothes and new shoes ready; scouting my opponents; advising me on strategy; being prepared for my postmatch routine, like stretching, drinking water, and getting some food inside me.

He also handled interview requests and public appearances organized by Kelly Wolf at my management firm, Octagon. He dealt with plane reservations. Called for transportation. Checked me into the hotel. When I think about what Carl has done to make my life more manageable over the years, it sounds incredible. I've overheard other coaches on the tour say, "Carl, I wouldn't want your job. You do so much more than a regular coach."

Not much escaped Carl's trained eye. Soon after he began coaching me, Carl noticed that I had a tendency to hold my racket a bit higher up the grip—a mild tennis version of choking up. Nearly all players, however, hold the racket at the end of the grip. Jim Courier and Andre Agassi hold their rackets *way* down the grip, right at the butt, which allows them to whip their rackets through the ball. I couldn't whip my racket because I was choking up.

Carl tried to get me to hold my racket lower, but I didn't feel good about it. We both knew, however, that it wasn't good for me to choke up on the racket. When that happened, I lost power and I lost reach, and every quarter-inch counted on the court.

Carl thought about it. "Well," he said, "we'll just have to make the racket longer."

Carl began an eighteen-month collaboration process with the Prince racket technicians and Bosworth International, experts in tuning, weighting, and balancing rackets. First, Carl asked Prince to add two inches to the frame. This may not sound like a lot, but in tennis terms, this was revolutionary. Rackets had been twenty-seven inches long ever since British Major Walter Clopton Wingfield decided to liven up an English garden party in 1873 with a game called "lawn tennis." Adding two inches to a twenty-seven-inch-long frame increased its length by 9 percent—a stunning amount.

We had to be careful. Although there were no restrictions on how long the racket could be (those would come *after* I started playing with a longer racket), you sacrificed maneuverability with a longer frame. You couldn't get the racket around for rapid-fire volleys, and what you gained in power, you subtracted in control.

I'll never forget the time when the first Longbody prototype arrived from the Prince R&D lab in New Jersey. Carl and I looked at these snowshoes, shared a laugh, and then decided to take them out for a spin. We played a set against each other, and the Longbody was powerful, all right: we served *bombs* to each other. The problem was that we couldn't return a serve if our lives depended on it, and on those rare occasions we managed to put a service return in play, Carl and I found it impossible to keep a rally going. I worried about hitting my forehand into the next area code.

"Carl, this is not going to work," I said after that frustrating episode.

"Yes, it will," he said. "Let me keep trying."

We went through more than a dozen prototypes. Carl orchestrated the entire process: he suggested new specs, play-tested each new prototype, and worked closely with the lab techs on the right materials. Carl knew Prince rackets, because since his junior days, he had played with each "new and improved" Prince model as it came off the assembly line: the Prince Boron, the Prince Woodie, the Prince Spectrum, the Prince Graphite—all of them.

I had played with the same frame—the Prince Graphite—for more than twelve years, so this would be a major change for me. The Prince Graphite had been a trusty sword ever since I first picked up the frame when I was ten years old—replacing my Prince Pro, an aluminum frame painted in black. I liked the way the stiffer Prince Graphite played, as well as its oversize shape. After playing thousands of hours with the Prince Graphite, the racket came to feel like an extension of my arm.

Not every Prince Graphite felt exactly alike, however. We asked the factory to modify the weight in the head of each frame, but even then, we noticed variances. Prince would send us a couple of dozen frames, and Carl would string up a dozen and play-test them.

"Michael, I don't want you to even waste your time with these," he said, pointing to a batch of cast-off frames. "They are totally off."

Carl took the same painstaking approach when it came to developing the Longbody. Until he thought he could give me something I could play with, he kept returning prototype after prototype to New Jersey—along with his feedback for ways to improve the frame. Since we both knew that the more powerful tennis rackets had tilted the playing field against me, Carl and I thought that maybe the Longbody could level things out on the court. After many months of testing, Carl thought we had the racket fine-tuned to the point where I could play with it during our Christmas break in 1993.

With the Longbody, he eventually shortened the racket from twenty-nine inches to twenty-eight inches before he finally developed one that he thought had the right weight and balance.

"Here, try this one out," he said. "I think we're there."

Carl was right: this was a frame I could play with. Not only did the extra inch give me greater reach, but I picked up ten to twenty miles per hour on my serve—a quantum leap for my game. Watch out, Pete Sampras: I was speeding at more than 120 mph.

"I like it," I said after an intense workout session with my brother. Not only did the Longbody serve like a rocket launcher, but my ground strokes were as solid as ever.

"I think we're on to something," Carl remarked. We both understood that if I could win one or two free points a game, I could regularly challenge—and beat—the top players: Sampras, Courier, and Agassi. Now, where had I heard those names before?

We knew the Longbody helped my serve, but what about my ground strokes? We couldn't afford any cracks in *that* foundation. I had to have total confidence when I whipped my forehand cross-court or attempted to hit my backhand down-the-line passing shot within an inch of where I wanted the ball to strike the court. We're talking precision because matches turn on how well you can "paint" the lines with your strokes.

After practicing with the new frame for only two weeks, we decided to give the Longbody a try at my first tournament of 1994 in Jakarta, Indonesia. We didn't tell anybody that I had new rackets in my bag, however. When the tournament started, I was more worried how the racket would play with my mind. I had always shrugged off poorly executed shots before, but what if I hit a poor shot or just missed with a passing shot? Would I wonder if it was the Longbody?

Once I stepped onto the court in Jakarta, my doubts were erased. I played well and won the tournament, but I still didn't say anything to the media. In fact, Carl and I were able to keep the wraps on the Longbody for another year or so while we continued to make small improvements in the frame. In the summer of 1995, the racket was released to the public with a huge marketing blitz from Prince. The Longbody became the world's best-selling racket for two years running in 1996 and 1997, despite a hefty price tag of $225.

AT THE SUMMIT

With the Longbody on top of the sales charts, I made my run for No. 1 as well. As mentioned before, I cracked the top 10 in 1992 after a three-year absence, with a ranking of No. 6. Life reached the whirlwind stage during this time. Because I was winning matches and going deeper into the draw, I was *playing* a lot of matches. It's one thing to lose in the second round on a Tuesday and have five days off before the next tournament; it's quite another to keep winning and playing into the weekend.

I'm not complaining. I loved staying busy and winning matches—and tournaments. From 1992 to 1997, I captured twenty-six of my thirty-four career titles. Many of those victories came at big tournaments in the U.S. and smaller tournaments in the Far East—Tokyo, Beijing, Shanghai, Kuala Lumpur, Osaka, Jakarta, and Hong Kong. I performed well in Asia because I always had the support of the local crowds. I also felt comfortable in that environment: I liked the food. I understood the Asian mentality. I felt at home. Success in Asia begat more success.

I also experienced more success in Grand Slam tournaments during this five-year span, and the good news was that I reached three finals: Roland Garros in 1995, the Australian Open in 1996, and the U.S. Open in 1996. The bad news: I lost all three chances to win a second Grand Slam.

It's an old tennis cliché that 126 other people would love to be in the shoes of two finalists when they stride out onto the court to play for a Grand Slam title before thousands of fans and a worldwide television audience. That is true. The anticipation and the exhilaration are an indescribable experience. Whether I was at Flinders Park, Roland Garros, or the United States Tennis Center, I could feel the buzz in the air, butterflies in my stomach, and the nervous tension, creating a rich experience.

On the final Sunday at a Grand Slam, there will be a winner and a loser. One will triumph in glory, and one will feel the bitter pain of defeat. While everyone on the tour knows that it's a tremendous feat just to get to the final two, the players are aware that the public doesn't remember who lost that day. Frank McGuire, a famous basketball coach, once said, "In this country, when you finish second, no one knows your name." There's a ring of truth to that statement. Win a Grand Slam title, and you make history. Lose, and you receive a silver plate and a nice check.

I reached three of the six Grand Slams finals played over the span of fifteen months. Let's take a closer look.

1995 FRENCH OPEN FINAL

It was no secret in the locker room that Thomas Muster (pronounced *Toe-mas Mooster*) liked to bully players. Maybe that was why he was nicknamed "the Terminator." If he could beat you through intimidation, he would do it. I didn't buy into that stuff. In previous matches, I ignored him and played my game as if to say, *I'm standing my ground, Thomas. I'm not going anywhere.*

This Austrian was one heck of a clay court player, however, and in 1995, he won twelve tournaments—all on clay. Thomas had a great spring leading up to the French. Nobody had beaten him in thirty-five matches on clay when we squared off at Court Central in the finals of Roland Garros, so he was a confident player. Thomas was also a grunter—a huffing machine who exerted great effort each time he pounded away at the ball. *Ah-huh*, he grunted, as if he was doing the clean-and-jerk with two hundred pounds. Sometimes grunters like Thomas fooled me; they let out this huge grunt and I would expect the ball to go shooting into the corner. All too often, the ball didn't have that much heat on it. Thomas had a peculiar "double grunt" in which he grunted just before he struck the ball and just after the ball left his strings. Weird. I had played grunters all my life, so it didn't bother me.

I started the match playing flawless tennis, taking the initiative all the way. Serving at 1–4, Thomas saved four break points, but I'm told that I missed a routine volley that would have given me a 5–1 lead. I've successfully forgotten *that* one. Later in the opening set, I had a 5–2 lead, but Thomas swept the next five games, and the momentum. I don't know what happened except that I lost control of a match that I had firmly within my grasp. Once Thomas saw that I was wounded, he grunted like an Olympic weight lifter as he began pummeling me with heavy topspin strokes. Re-energized and reborn, Thomas played like a man on a mission to win a Grand Slam that he had dreamed of winning ever since he was a small boy.

1996 Australian Open Final

When Boris Becker and I squared off in Melbourne for the Australian championship in early 1996, the twenty-eight-year-old German star hadn't won a Grand Slam in five years. When we walked onto the court to start the match, we stood together at the net for the ceremonial photos prior to the coin toss. I looked over at Boris, who stood six-feet, three-inches. I decided to have a little fun. I stood on my tippy toes while the cameras clicked away. Boris noticed what everyone was grinning about, so *he* stood on his toes.

Boris didn't play head and shoulders better than I, but man, did he play superbly in the final. Then again, Boris always matched up well against me, and I only beat him once in the three or four times we played each other during our careers. When Boris is going for his shots and making them, it's tough to get him off his game. What can I say? Boris's best days may have been behind him, but he played brilliantly at Flinders Park—and made several signature diving volleys on big points. "To tell you the truth, I didn't think I had a Grand Slam left in me," Boris told the sellout crowd during his victory speech.

I wish I had known that three hours ago, I thought. One reason I think Boris played so well is because he wanted his wife, Barbara, to witness him winning a Grand Slam. (His previous five Slam titles came before they met.)

1996 U.S. Open Final

Back in the days when I played Nerf tennis in my Minnesota basement as a first-grader, I imagined winning Wimbledon. Perhaps that's because the green lawns of Centre Court seemed so magical and so far away, or because the thought of the Duchess of Kent handing me the Wimbledon trophy while I bowed seemed too surreal. Anyway, as my tennis career progressed, the tournament I *really* wanted to win became the U.S. Open.

Part of it had to do with being an American and growing up playing tennis in this country. Another reason is because I had such warm fan support whenever I played at Flushing Meadow. I liked being a hometown favorite instead of feeling like a foreigner in London, Paris, or Melbourne. To be sure, I had plenty of family and relatives cheering me on each time I returned to New York City. I wanted to do them proud and lift the U.S. Open trophy one time.

Up until 1996, the U.S. Open had been a mental challenge. I often played dramatic matches on big occasions, but it always seemed that I was *this* close to breaking through. I seemed to run into and lose to the eventual winner a lot: Stefan Edberg in 1992, Pete Sampras in 1993, and Andre Agassi in 1994.

For the 1996 U.S. championship, I exacted revenge by defeating Andre in a straight-set semifinal wipeout on Super Saturday. Waiting for me in the finals was another old, old rival: Pete Sampras. We were the No. 1 and No. 3 players in the world, and if I could beat Pete, I would supplant him and reach the rarefied air of No. 1 for the first time in my career.

There was a lot at stake playing for No. 1, and it seemed like every other person reminded me of that fact. I warmed up about ninety minutes before our 4 P.M. start time, but then a drenching thunderstorm swept through the USTA Tennis Center, causing a rain delay. I knew it would be at least a couple of hours before we could play, so I found a couch in the locker room and snoozed for an hour.

I chose not to go out and warm up again after my nap. Instead, I stretched and jumped some rope. I felt ready since I had already hit that day, but I think if I had warmed up a second time, I would have been able to see where I was adrenaline-wise. You see, when I walked onto Louis Armstrong Court in front of twenty thousand spectators, I was wound *way* too tight. The enormity of playing the "biggest match of my career" caused me to start out way too pumped up. With my intensity tachometer registering beyond the redline, I wasn't able to properly channel my energies into playing a calm, reasoned, and focused match. I needed a level head, not a hopped-up beginning.

Like a balloon losing its air, I came out flat in the first set. I didn't get settled until the middle of the second set, but I was already down a break, and one thing you don't want to do is give Pete Sampras a two-set lead in a money match. But that's exactly what happened. If Pete had shown anything during his remarkable career, it was the ability to play at a high level when the circumstances demanded his best.

Late in the third set, I had my opportunities. I had a set point at 5–6, but my forehand clipped the net and sat up for Pete, who drilled a forehand cross-court while I approached the net. I stabbed at his passing shot and got the ball on my racket, but it hit the tape.

That would be my only chance. Within a few minutes, Pete closed out a match that had been an emotional seesaw for him as well. His coach, Tim Gullikson, had died of cancer a few months earlier, so when Pete won the final point, he raised his arms in triumph and looked to the sky. Everyone, including myself, understood what he was trying to say: *This is for you, buddy.*

I congratulated Pete and thought of what might have been. My dream of winning the U.S. Open and reaching No. 1 would have to wait until another day.

• OFF-SEASON KARATE TRAINING •

—— • ——

CHAPTER 8

THE SUDDEN SLIDE

L ike a mountain climber forced to turn back after coming within one hundred feet of Mt. Everest's summit, I had to deal with disappointment, the what-ifs and what-could-I-have-done-betters? I decided, following prayer and reflection, to mount another assault on the Grand Slams and try to reach the game's pinnacle in 1997. After hopscotching between No. 2 and No. 3 in the world for most of the year, I entered the 1997 U.S. Open with a foothold on No. 2, ready to take another crack at you-know-who: Pete Sampras.

The computer that calculated the rankings, however, told us that even if I won the tournament, I could not overtake Pete at the U.S. Open. But if I won Flushing Meadow and had a strong fall, I could end the 1997 campaign at No. 1.

On the tournament's first day, the USTA dedicated its new Arthur Ashe Stadium, a $254 million tennis palace that seated twenty-three thousand. Forty former champions paraded onto the Ashe Stadium court for the dedication ceremony. As I watched the event unfold on

TV back at my hotel, I must confess to the sin of envy. I wanted to be out there, standing shoulder to shoulder with the legends of the game: Don Budge, Rod Laver, Ken Rosewall, John Newcombe, Billie Jean King, Martina Navratilova, and Monica Seles, to name a few. I noticed that my old buddy Ivan Lendl, who had retired after the 1994 season, had a big grin on his face.

I won my first five rounds and arrived at Super Saturday and the men's semifinals with an unusual circumstance: Pete and Andre and Jim were out, and Boris Becker and Stefan Edberg had left the building due to retirement. I was the highest-ranked player left in the field. Suddenly I was the *favorite*.

This development caused the media spotlight to swing in my direction, and I noticed more TV and print journalists showing up at my press conferences. Following one of my meet-the-media sessions, Bill Simons, the publisher of *Inside Tennis* (a regional tennis periodical published in California), asked whether he could have a private word with me.

I had known Bill since my junior days, so I nodded yes, and we slipped into a corridor for a quick stand-up. Bill said that he had heard me mention the Bible in the pressroom, so he was wondering, "Who is your favorite character in the Bible?"

I *liked* that question. I thought about saying Job, the richest cattleman in the land of Uz who lost everything—seven thousand sheep, three thousand camels, five hundred teams of oxen, plus his ten children and his health—before being restored by God. The book of Job is a story of one man's incredible perseverance and unshakable faith in God.

But Job isn't my favorite character in the Bible—David is. Warming to the topic, I talked at length about how David—a teenage boy who witnessed a nine-foot-tall giant named Goliath taunting the army of

Israel and defying their God—rose to the challenge. David told Goliath prior to their face-off that he was coming at him in the name of the Lord, and that he would kill him that day as proof that the Lord works without regard to human means. Most of us know what happened next. David reached into his shepherd's bag, took out a flat stone, and hurled it from his sling. The stone struck Goliath in the forehead, and the giant toppled to the ground. David ran over, pulled Goliath's sword from his sheath, and killed him with it, causing the Israelites to defeat their hated enemy, the Philistines. David's story resonated with me because everyone told him that he was too small, too young, and too inexperienced to take on a towering, battle-scarred veteran like Goliath. Yet the young boy was victorious because he believed the Lord was with him and that he was doing God's will.

I noticed Bill taking notes, but I'm not sure if our discussion ever landed in print. A year later, however, I ran into Bill at the U.S. Open again, and I could tell that he wanted to unburden something from his heart. We met for another one-on-one in the corridor. "Michael, if it's okay," he began, "I would like to tell you about something that happened to me just after we spoke last year at this tournament."

I nodded for him to proceed. I listened as Bill described how a few weeks after the U.S. Open, he had visited with his ailing mother, Edna Simons, who was on her deathbed. They were making small talk, and Bill told her about his conversation with me regarding David and the Bible. His mother's eyes lit up, and she asked her son to read the story of David from 1 Samuel in the Old Testament. Bill said that this was the last meaningful conversation he had with his mother; she died the following day.

As Bill related the story, tears came to his eyes as he recalled the love of his mother. When it looked as though he could not continue, I said, "Take your time. I know this is difficult for you." It became an emotional moment for both of us, and I gave him a pat on the back and told him I would be praying for him.

I could have used some prayer myself in my next match against Patrick Rafter in the 1997 U.S. Open semifinals. Patrick is one of the talents on tour who had flirted with several breakthrough moments during his career. With his long, black hair pulled tightly back in a ponytail, Patrick cut quite a swath on the court. He served big and volleyed even bigger, coming in behind nearly everything.

I stood my ground against Patrick's serving barrage, but the Aussie outplayed me that afternoon, winning in three straight sets. After he won match point, I walked up to the net for the postmatch handshake. I was supremely disappointed, but Patrick had played honorably. "I hope you win this one," I said, as I looked Patrick in the eye and took his hand. "You're playing great."

The loss hit my family hard because we thought the draw had opened up in my favor for a change. Since my match was the last one of Super Saturday, the capacity crowd filed out of Arthur Ashe Stadium. There's a memorable shot of Carl, sitting alone in the family box in an empty stadium, staring straight ahead, forlorn in his thoughts, wondering what might have been. Already, he was formulating a strategy to take me to the summit of the men's game.

ROCKY REVISITED

One of the universal complaints among the players is the absence of an off-season. The tennis year usually begins a few hours after fireworks ring in the New Year, with warm-up tournaments leading up to the Australian Open in the last two weeks of January. Then it's back to the U.S. for several indoor events, followed by Indian Wells and Miami. Then we're off to Europe for the clay court season, which runs into the French Open in late May and early June. Following Paris, we jump over to grass for two weeks of preparation prior to Wimbledon. After six to eight weeks in Europe, we can finally come home for a break—but not too long. We have the North American summer season (Los Angeles, Toronto or Montreal, Cincinnati, and Washington, D.C.), which takes us right into the U.S. Open. Then I move into my hectic fall schedule—usually a series of tournaments in the Far East and Europe. When my year is tabulated, I'm on the road an average of thirty-two weeks a year.

The only break we can count on is from the middle of November to New Year's Day—unless we are playing in a Davis Cup final. In 1997, I spent Thanksgiving week in Goteborg, Sweden, playing for the United States against Sweden—and wished I hadn't. Pete got injured, I lost my opening match to Jonas Bjorkman, and the U.S. was swept 5–0. When I arrived in Henderson, Nevada, a Las Vegas suburb where I had been making my home for the last six or seven years, I was running on fumes. The year 1997 had been my most intense on the tour, especially because I had played a strong fall schedule. I finalized the year at No. 3; Patrick Rafter, who went on to win his first Grand Slam at the U.S. Open, beat me out for the second spot in the year-end rankings.

This slight slip fueled a desire to work harder during my off-season and make 1998 my best year ever and hopefully break through to No. 1. Carl had been plotting ways to make me stronger, figuring that was the missing piece of the puzzle. As we discussed his plans following my return from Sweden, Carl knew that my body usually required ten days to two weeks to recuperate. He understood why I needed to recharge my batteries—physically, mentally, and emotionally—and that fishing together at Lake Mead was often the right tonic.

This time, however, Carl shared a bold plan to increase my strength and quickness. "Unfortunately, that means you get only four days off," said my brother and coach.

"Four days?" I replied. We both knew that I needed four days just to recover from jet lag. "Are you sure?"

"If we're going to make you stronger, yes," said Carl.

I was so tired that I didn't even fish on my four-day mini-vacation. I just laid around the house that I shared with Carl and his wife, Diana, watching a little TV and catching up on my reading.

What happened over the next five weeks is something I bought into. Nobody forced me to work as physically hard as I did. Although Carl devised this training regimen, I had veto power at any time. I thought that working my body as hard as I did was the price I had to fork over to reach my goal of winning more Grand Slams and becoming No. 1.

Six days a week, I pulled my tired body out of bed at 6 A.M. and jogged for a half hour as the sun rose up over the desert landscape. Carl and I ran around the perimeter of our subdivision, which was called Quail Ridge. After that eye-opener, we returned home. I knew what was next—twenty minutes of jumping rope. I skipped and jumped rope in five-minute sets, resting for two minutes between each set. After cooling off, I ate a little breakfast—rice or leftovers from the night before, maybe some eggs. I usually only eat cereal when I'm on the road or in a rush. As I recall, my parents were visiting at the time, so Mom or Dad probably cooked up something warm for me.

We also had another visitor staying with us, a karate instructor whom we addressed as Huang Jiao-lian. He was introduced to us by a friend of Carl's. Huang Jiao-lian put me through an intense, ninety-minute karate workout with explosive kicks and animated punches. This was not my first exposure to karate; I had taken lessons in Placentia before the 1989 French Open. My energetic instructor worked me pretty hard, but that was to be expected because karate is an exact discipline. He wanted me to perform the moves correctly while maintaining respect for the art of karate. Although the workouts were arduous, I enjoyed them because I was learning self-defense and certain movements. The goal was to bring me to an orange belt status—roughly the midway point in the hierarchy of belts.

Carl joined me for the karate lessons and mimicked each power move, which helped since I found it easier to work with someone. When the morning lesson was over, I took a two-hour break. Actually, I used the time to rest up for what we were going to do *after* lunchtime.

We picked things up at one o'clock with another ninety minutes of karate, perfecting the moves that we'd worked on in the morning. Following that intense session, Carl and I hopped in the car and drove over to the Green Valley Athletic Club (now known as the Sports Club/Las Vegas), a big club with indoor courts, outdoor courts, an indoor swimming pool, indoor track, racquetball, and a well-equipped weight room.

It was the weight room where I did my best "Rocky" imitation. In the original movie, Rocky did these rat-a-tat pull-ups; when I started working with weights after Sweden, I could barely do one. But after a month of bench presses and squats, increasing the weight with each series of repetitions, and making the rounds with the Nautilus machines, I could hang free and crank out fifteen of those pull-ups. *Getting stronger . . .*

Carl and I pumped iron in the weight room for a good two hours following my afternoon karate lesson. When we were finished lifting barbells and pushing plates, we drove home for some rest and relaxation. Training wasn't over, however. After dinner, I would do what I call "mirror work": swinging a racket in the living room, making forehand and backhand movements while I watched my form in a large mirror. This half-hour-long footwork drill was the equivalent of shadowboxing.

I didn't have much left in the tank, so I showered, relaxed a bit, and fell into bed only to start another long day of physical work in the morning. The only time I rested was on the seventh day—the Sabbath. For each glorious Sunday, I slept in and attended the 10:30 service at Central Christian Church with my family. After the service, we feasted on fine Chinese food at one of our favorite restaurants. When we got home, there wasn't much daylight left since it was December. That meant no time for fishing at Lake Mead.

Like I said, it was Carl's idea to ratchet things up in the fitness area. We both knew that I had always been one of the fittest players on the tour, but after the Rafter loss, we both felt that I shouldn't have been as tired as I had been going into the semifinals. Yes, I had to fight through back-to-back five-setters to get to Patrick, but my fatigue cost me the match—and perhaps the U.S. Open title. The thinking in our camp was that I needed to get stronger so that I would be able to recover better between matches. Hence, the Henderson boot camp over five weeks.

Simultaneously, we were starting to see more and more big servers out there; guys like Krajicek, Ivanisevic, Rafter, and Rusedski were carpet-bombing the courts. Everyone I ran up against seemed to be playing this version of power tennis. When guys serve really hard, there's a difference between being able to block the return back or being able to control how you hit the return. I needed to get stronger so that when a big serve came my way, my racket wasn't affected by it. I had to be strong enough to overcome the pace on the ball and return the serve where I wanted to. God had blessed me with speed, quickness, and agility, but I needed to work on power. The time to do it was now, since in a few months I would turn twenty-six years old—probably the prime of my tennis career.

A New Year Approaching

We have a Christmas Eve tradition in the Chang family, a tradition that began when we moved out to California when I was seven years old. Every December 24, all our Southern California relatives come to our house, or we travel to Aunt Nancy's home in Thousand Oaks, for fellowship and a time of prayer. A buffet table brims with wonderful Chinese dishes, and we eat like it's Thanksgiving. For Christmas 1997, everyone gathered at Aunt Nancy's. My grandparents were there, along with Mom and Dad, Carl and Diana, and my cousins Joe, Jimmy, Jerry, Jessica, Ben, Lynn, Bing, and Don—around twenty in all.

After enjoying our wonderful meal, we sang Christmas carols and praise songs, and then we had a time to share what the Lord had been doing in our lives and things we needed prayer for. I had always looked forward to this special time because it meant so much to have my family behind me in prayer. When it was my turn to speak, I noticed everyone's eyes fixed in my direction.

"It's been tough to come so close," I began, "but now that 1998 is coming around, I think it's going to be an unbelievable year. I've worked really, really hard and prepared well for the coming season, and

I can't wait to get started. I ask for your prayers for guidance and wisdom since I am on the road a lot. I ask for a certain humility so God can do all that He wants to do through me and what He wants to accomplish."

Our prayer time that evening was an emotional one. As we bowed our heads in prayer, we knew that God cares about every little detail of our lives, and that prayer is an incredible source of power.

A NEW CAMPAIGN

Shortly after New Year's Day, we flew down to Australia for the start of the new campaign. First up was an eight-man exhibition event at the Kooyong Tennis Club in Melbourne. I was playing a practice set against Mark Philippoussis one day when I went to hit a serve. I immediately felt a sharp pain in my rib cage. I stopped playing and sought a trainer, who, upon examination, said I had strained the muscle attachment to my rib.

I nursed the muscle strain into the Australian Open, but I didn't feel like my old self when I lost in straight sets to the Frenchman Guillaume Raoux in the second round. Naturally, the disappointment was keen since I had been a finalist two years earlier and came into the tournament as the third seed. I had an easier time swallowing the early-round loss, however, because I knew I was injured.

I felt well enough to return to the tour for the Kroger St. Jude in Memphis, where I got back on track and reached the finals. I lost to Philippoussis, known as "Scud" by the players for the missiles he launches every time he makes a service toss. During our match, however, I noticed a heel bruise, but I dismissed it as one of those nagging injuries. The heel bruise worsened to the point where I was limping between points.

I took the week off after Memphis and flew to Palm Springs, where my parents have a vacation home. I had a week to recover and ready myself for Indian Wells—the Newsweek Champions Cup. Tournament director Charlie Pasarell puts on a great tournament, and I've had great success there in the past, winning three times. As I prepared for the 1998 event, I was the defending two-time champion.

On the Thursday before the tournament start date, I was practicing with Andrei Medvedev, a top Russian player, at the Hyatt Grand Champions tennis complex. We were playing on an outside court, not one of the "show courts." The surface was hard court, but adjacent to us was a clay court.

Andrei and I were playing a practice set in the late afternoon, around five o'clock. I noticed that someone had turned on the sprinklers to wet down the clay court next to us. *Chit . . . chit . . . chit.* When a twilight desert breeze passed by the courts, I felt some moisture on my forehead.

Andrei and I had been playing for more than an hour in the desert sun, so I welcomed the cooling spray from the court next door. At 6–5, I reached set point in our practice match. Andrei came in on a short ball and poked a little drop volley toward my forehand side. I immediately sprinted toward the ball, hoping to get there before it bounced twice. This was something I had done thousands of times in my career. I ran six, seven, and eight steps before planting with my right foot and sliding into the shot while I took a forehand swing. When I planted, however, I felt my right foot slip underneath me, so I overcompensated to keep my balance while hitting the ball. All this motion placed tremendous stress on my left knee—and then I heard something pop. I somehow managed to keep my balance while hitting the ball for a winner and the set!

It turned out to be a costly victory. Once the point was over, I couldn't walk, and that's when I became really concerned. Carl hustled over to the tournament office, and within minutes a golf cart with a flat bed—like the ones you see carting off an injured football player—arrived on the scene. They transported me to a waiting van, where I was driven to the Desert Orthopedic Center in Rancho Mirage. Dr. Sam Reber, the tournament doctor, was waiting to see me.

I recognized the doctor's face, which helped to calm my nerves. "Good to see you again, Michael," said Dr. Reber, "although not under these circumstances. What do we have here?" he asked, as he peered at my left knee.

"I'm not sure," I replied. "I hurt it slipping on a wet court." I explained how the gentle mist from the sprinklers on the clay court next door had also moistened a section of *our* court just past the doubles alley.

"We better have an MRI done," said Dr. Reber. While we waited for that to happen, I remembered the last time I had seen the tournament doctor. A few years earlier, I went to Dr. Reber with a large boil on my chest.

"Michael, I'm going to have to lance it," he had announced.

"Fine." Then I noticed that after he washed his hands, Dr. Reber did not put any surgical gloves on. That was weird. Even my dentist wore gloves to protect himself against various infections, so I attempted to allay any fears that he might harbor in treating me. "You don't have anything to worry about, Doctor. I don't have AIDS or anything like that."

"Michael, I'm not worried about that because I know your lifestyle. I know you're a Christian."

"Are you a Christian too?"

"Yes, I am."

Now Dr. Reber escorted me to the magnetic resonance imaging room, where an MRI confirmed his gut diagnosis: I had partially torn my medial collateral ligament—the MCL—in my left knee. I would not be defending my title in Indian Wells.

"The good news is that you will not need surgery," said Dr. Reber. "You need to rest that knee."

"How long do I have to stay off the courts?"

"One, two weeks, maybe a month."

Dr. Reber handed me a pair of crutches and a knee brace, and counseled me to make good use of them. Hobbling around on crutches really made me feel injured, and I did not like that feeling at all. I took it easy for a week or two and then flew to Miami, where I hoped to play in the Lipton. I ditched the crutches, and when I felt I could move well enough, I returned to the practice court with Carl to see where I stood. Whenever I hit forehands or moved to my right side, I had no problems since I was hitting off my right leg. Whenever I hit backhands or moved to my left side—and pushed off on my left knee—I was definitely compromised and would feel a great deal of pain. Moving around the court with a brace around my left knee felt as if I were dragging a two-pound sack of flour.

I still wanted to play, so I left my name in the draw and decided to wait until the last moment to see whether the knee would come around. I warmed up an hour before my first-round match. Carl and I sized up the situation: I could still move well to my forehand, but I experienced plenty of pain moving to my backhand side. Despite this assessment, I still wanted to play my match against Christian Vinck of Germany. That's how stubborn I was.

I had been seeing the Lipton tournament doctor, Dr. Charles Virgin, for several days, and after my warm-up, he found me in the locker room.

"What do you think?" asked Dr. Virgin.

"I think I'm going to give it a try," I said.

"Michael, listen to me. I enjoy your tennis too much, and I don't want to see you get hurt. I think you are making a mistake if you go out and play. Tell you what. I'm going to make the decision for you. I'm not clearing you to play."

"Really?" Normally, if you say you're okay, the doctors shrug their shoulders and sign you off. Not Dr. Virgin.

"That's what I'm saying. I can't let you play."

I returned to our condo, where Carl was waiting with a portable ultrasound treatment machine from Dynatron. Carl, a self-taught physical therapist, had done some research. He put on his PT hat and treated me several times a day with electronic stimulation. I returned to Henderson for more rehab. Looming on my calendar was a two-week trip to Asia for a pair of tournaments and appearances. The fans there—as well as my sponsors—were expecting me.

I decided to make the long flight to Hong Kong, the first stop. My left knee, trussed up in the heavy brace, still hurt a fair amount. After practicing several times, I decided to tape the knee as well. Weighted down like a medieval knight in armor, I couldn't run very well. Ironically, I had drawn Christian Vinck again in the first round, and this time we actually played the match. Christian won in three sets—a match I could have won if I had decent wheels. This development annoyed and frustrated me.

"Carl, I can't move with this brace," I said annoyingly to my coach and brother.

"You're going to have to give it time, Michael."

"Forget it. I'm not wearing this brace anymore."

I took off the brace and prepared for my next tournament in Tokyo. I don't know how, but I managed to win my first-round match. However, Hendrik Dreekmann, a German player, had done some asking around in the locker room prior to our second-round encounter. When he heard that I had the mobility of a senior player, he started drop-shotting me from the first game.

After about the third drop shot five minutes into the match, I whispered to myself, "Uh-oh." I hustled my buns off as Hendrik hit me into the corner and then tapped a drop shot to the other side of the court. I kept things close in this three-set loss, but I knew that I needed a skateboard to run down those balls.

I left Asia for home, where the knee finally responded to Dynatron stimulation and treatment from the ATP trainers. Tiger Balm also helped, but the knee continued to bug me—although it wasn't enough to keep me off the courts. I continued to play a full schedule, losing to Jim Courier in the finals of the U.S. Clay Court Championships at Disney World. Then I traveled to Rome, where I was encouraged when I beat Pete Sampras in the second round of the Italian Open. I also outserved the greatest server in the history of the game—eleven aces to five! But now a *new* problem surfaced—my left wrist. That wrist got so sore that I couldn't hit a normal two-handed backhand. The trainer said it was tendonitis.

My quarterfinal match was against Albert Costa of Spain, a very tough clay courter. During my warm-up with Carl, I couldn't hit a two-handed backhand.

"What am I going to do?" I asked Carl.

He didn't have an answer. I tried playing anyway, and since I didn't have a backhand, I ran around and hit all forehands, doing my best imitation of Thomas Muster. I'm sure I gave the boys in the locker room something to talk about: *Did you see Chang running around his backhand today?* That style of play opened up the court on my forehand side, which Albert took advantage of. He made me run eight, ten, and twelve steps to cover my forehand side. When Albert hit back to my backhand side, all I could do was poke the ball with a one-handed slice. I felt like a sitting duck in winning only three games against the Spaniard.

PRIVATE THOUGHTS

It was easy to turn introspective at this downturn in my career. Prior to 1998, I experienced plenty of short-term ups and downs in ten years on the tour, but the general trend remained upward. Sure, I didn't win every tournament, but I was certainly in the hunt at many of the tour stops.

One sure thing about playing professional tennis is that there is plenty of waiting around—in player lounges, airport terminals, and hotel rooms. In a desire to do something useful with this downtime, I decided to start writing in a journal in 1991.

I wrote, all right. In a bedside drawer at home are journals containing my most private thoughts over the past ten years. I wrote these out by longhand until I purchased my first laptop computer a few years ago. Sometimes I write about my tennis or my social life, but more often than not, I write what is on my mind or what the Lord places on my heart. Naturally, some of what I have written is too private to disclose, but I'm going to share a few entries in this chapter.

Over the years, I have learned that when the Lord wants to show me something, He wakes me up. This happens in the middle of the night, or sometimes during an afternoon nap—times when I am *tired*. No matter. I rub my eyes and say, *All right, Lord,* and I pull my tired frame out of bed.

I begin by praying and then reading some passage from the Bible. Then I pray again, and sudden thoughts will hit me. I've come to learn that God is trying to say something to me. That's when I begin writing my innermost thoughts. Following the Italian Open and my subsequent loss in Hamburg, I typed this entry into my laptop:

> *May 9, 1998:* The Lord spoke to me a few nights ago. In fact, I couldn't sleep at all, so I felt He wanted to tell me something. He gave me Philippians 3:14: "I press on toward the goal to win the prize for which God has called me heavenward in Christ Jesus."
>
> Before, I never could understand that verse. What is the goal? The goal is to know God. It's not winning Grand Slams, or being No. 1, or finding a wife. It's knowing God. Really knowing Him. Doing what you know He wants you to do. Being obedient even if you know it's difficult. But taking the time to really know Him. Then your care and focus will be on what is good and perfect—and that's Him—and not on worldly things that only eat away at you if you don't attain them. I feel like I have a bigger purpose—the best purpose—now, and that is truly knowing Him.

That was my mind-set as I entered the French Open. Now I was receiving treatment for my left knee *and* left wrist. Ice, ultrasound, massage—I tried it all. It soon became apparent that I couldn't ask the ATP trainers to spend hours treating me—that wasn't fair to the rest of the play-ers. So we decided to hire Nalini Advani, a trainer I had met at the Hong Kong event, to treat me for the rest of the summer or however long it took.

Paris turned out to be another frustrating experience, where I lost in the third round to Francisco Clavet of Spain. I was the last American to go out, but that offered little solace. I flew back to Southern California with my parents and Nalini. We drove to Camarillo, located between Los Angeles and Santa Barbara, to meet with a renowned hand surgeon. He had operated on Andre Agassi after the 1993 season when it looked like he had a career-ending wrist injury.

The doctor examined my wrist. "I've done this type of surgery a thousand times," he said. "It's no problem."

He read the look of skepticism on my face. "Really, I'll have you back on the court in no time, just like Andre."

I'm the kind of person who goes under the knife only as a last resort. In fact, the only time I had submitted to surgery was when my wisdom teeth were yanked out in tenth grade—four days before I took my GED test.

I was reluctant for two reasons:

1. You never know what will happen in the operating room. One little slip with the scalpel, and my tennis career would be *finito*.

2. Wrist surgery would knock me out of the U.S. Open.

When I sought God's will about this surgery, I didn't feel at peace. This doctor, however, was a strong advocate for surgery and was almost too con-fident for my taste. I did not call back for a follow-up appointment.

When I resumed playing, Carl started having me dump my left hand into a bucket of ice water after each match and practice session to numb the inflamed nerves in the wrist. Still the wrist couldn't hack it.

That summer, I pulled out of tournaments, played in some, and tried my best to cope. I reached the quarterfinals in Washington, D.C., where I ran into Jim Courier again. Whenever Jim and I played, I mentally brought a lunch bucket to the court because I knew we were going to bash balls all day long. Jim liked to hit the ball hard, and I liked to counterpunch. The matchup often produced many crowd-pleasing rallies and tough points. Fortunately, I prevailed that day, but my tender wrist was so sore afterward that I couldn't hit a ball before my semifinal match against Scott Draper the next afternoon, so I pulled out even before a ball was struck.

I took another break to give the wrist time to heal, and it finally started to come around. This is what I typed in my journal while I played the ATP Championships in Cincinnati:

August 12, 1998: My wrist felt great in yesterday's match against Todd Woodbridge, and I praise the Lord for taking care of it. When we were driving home, I noticed the sun and its rays shining down upon the earth, and I knew the beauty of witnessing that with the Lord's light and love shining upon me. How wonderful my God is.

After a tough, three-set loss to Yevgeny Kafelnikov, I wrote these words:

August 13, 1998: It's 1:49 a.m. I praise the Lord for continuing to take care of my wrist. I lost today, but I had no pain in the wrist. I've been praying for the Lord's wisdom and guidance as far as what to do, even surgery, and now He is revealing to me that surgery is something I don't need to think about right now. I thank Him so much for that.

Later that month in a tournament in Boston, I made a nice run again. In my semifinal victory against Sebastien Grosjean of France, however, I strained my groin and hamstring muscles right where the muscles meet. I remember being in the locker room with Dad, Nalini, and Carl. My father asked me how I was feeling.

"Not good," I replied. "I'm having a hard time changing directions. I can feel pain where I strained those muscles."

Nagging injury after nagging injury finally had caused Dad's frustration level to come to a boil. "Gosh, I can't believe you got hurt again!" he fulminated. "How many times this whole year have we had to deal with you getting hurt?" I had never seen Dad so worked up.

"You know, Baba," I said, using my term of endearment, "we've been through all these things, and the Lord has always taken care of everything. This is just another thing that we shall have to deal with. Everything's going to be fine."

"But what's going to happen tomorrow? Are you going to play hurt?"

"I'm going to be okay, Baba." For some reason, I had some assurance. "With all the injuries I've been through this whole year, we can be assured that the Lord will take care of it."

When I played in the finals against Paul Haarhuis, a Dutch player, I didn't feel much pain at all in defeating him. The wrist was manageable, as well, in winning my first tournament of the year. It felt great to return to the winner's circle and raised my hopes going into the U.S. Open.

At Flushing Meadow I played probably one of the most frustrating matches of my career in the second round. I had drawn Carlos Moya of Spain—a dangerous player who had won the French Open a few months earlier. After winning the first two sets, I had Carlos down match point late in the third. He spun in a serve to my backhand, and

I ripped the ball down the line. All both of us could do was watch and wait for the call because my shot either hit part of the line or was out by an inch. "Out!" screamed the line judge. My shoulders sank, and so did my fortunes. Granted a reprieve, Carlos came back to beat me in five sets, which was only the second time in my career that I blew a two-set-to-love lead.

It took me a week to shake off that match, but I bounced back by winning Shanghai in early October. Then I lost in the first round in Singapore and wrote this in my journal:

> October 18, 1998: It's 12:53 a.m. right now, and it's so quiet. I really love times like this because it takes me away from the hustle and bustle of life. But even more important, it is times like these that the Lord speaks to me. I have been able to learn quite a bit over the past ten days, particularly about listening to God. My prayer life has always been me doing the talking, but after reading a few chapters of Too Busy Not to Pray, I have learned how important it is to be still and quiet. The Lord speaks most often to me in a gentle voice, and now I am learning to listen more during my prayer time.
> It has been good.

Things started to jell in my mind about *why* I was traveling through this "desert" experience. I had dropped from No. 3 to No. 29 in the world in twelve months.

> October 28, 1998: I believe I am starting to understand a little bit better why things have happened the way they have

the past year. Obviously, there is spiritual warfare, growing of faith, and growing in my trust in the Lord. The one thing that stood out a bit more recently than all the others is the concept of letting go. Letting my tennis go out of my hands and into His.

As I reflect upon last year's off-season, the time where I worked so hard for five weeks straight, I realize that what I did was really wrong. It was wrong not to rest. Wrong to not even relax and go fishing. And it was wrong to think I could accomplish my tennis goals in my own strength.

Look what has happened this year. The Lord has opened my eyes to this, and He wants me to be balanced in hard work and in the way I rest and play. He wants me to trust Him. To let go of my dreams so that He can fulfill His realities, His plan, and I praise the Lord for showing me this.

It's so hard to let go. But quite honestly, I have tried everything else, and it's taken a year like this to make me do it. But I'm happy about it because I know the Lord only wants the best for me. How awesome He is.

So there you have it. I had tried to get to No. 1 on *my* strength, instead of depending on the Lord to take me to the game's summit, if that was His will. In other words, going *way* beyond the normal training methods by working my body from sunup to sundown was not honoring what the Lord could do in my life. I was not *trusting* in Him. It was as if David went to do battle with Goliath, but to cover his bases, he packed a pistol in his shepherd's bag *just* in case his slingshot did not do the trick.

TURNING A CORNER

Following the 1998 season, I took a six-week break to rest my weary body. *I'm listening, Lord.* My left wrist was still bothering me, so I decided not to do anything for two weeks—not even carry a plastic bag of groceries in my left hand. Then I tried a treatment called iontophoresis every other day for a half hour. It's hard to describe, but basically I wet a pad with a cortical steroid and used electrical current to drive it in. I did eight treatments over two weeks, and after that my wrist pain was gone!

I was kicking myself, but nonetheless, I was thankful to the Lord. He had relieved me of a constant, drip, drip kind of pain. It felt almost unreal to feel 100 percent.

I anticipated when I could start hitting balls again. "Carl, this is fantastic," I gushed. "My wrist feels great." Something else happened in 1998 to make me feel bullish about my future, although I didn't know that the worst was yet to come.

• TEAM CHANG •
MOM AND BABY KATIE, CARL, DIANA, DAD, AND ME

———— • ————

CHAPTER 9

MAKING THE MOVE

I n the midst of my tennis career taking an interesting turn in 1998, there were interesting developments off court: I moved.

Let me begin by laying all the pieces on the table. A year or so after winning the French Open in 1989, there was enough money in the bank to buy a nicer home, so we moved to Coto de Caza, a lovely community near Mission Viejo. When Carl became my coach in 1991, Mom and Dad continued to live in the Coto de Caza house while I purchased a home in Henderson, Nevada, for Carl and me. Henderson is located about a half-hour's drive from Lake Mead, a fantastic striped-bass fishery and a wonderful place to relax.

Carl and I enjoyed being around each other, and we found that living together made sense—until Carl fell in love with a beautiful young woman he had met when he was attending Cal Berkeley. Her name was Diana Ying, and they were married in December 1995. Diana began traveling with us everywhere and quickly became part of the Chang Gang. We continued to share our home in Henderson because we spent many more days on the road than at home sweet home in Quail Ridge.

Not surprisingly, Carl and Diana began talking about starting a family. When children come along, that changes the household dynamics, so Carl and Diana planned to eventually move into a place of their own. That was understandable. As we began discussing our options, we squarely faced some questions:

- Is Henderson where Carl and Diana wanted to raise a family? And what about myself? Remember, I had aspirations of marrying and having a family as well.
- If Henderson is not where we see each other staying long-term, where would we want to move?

At the end of the day, we didn't want to raise our children in the gambling environment that pervades Las Vegas and Nevada, where slot machines are found in supermarkets and Keno sheets are handed out with restaurant menus. As for the heat, let's just say that you notice the blast furnace summers more when you live in Henderson year-round, instead of bopping in and out like we did—the traveling nomads.

If not Henderson, where could we move? Our new home had to satisfy several criteria:

- We had to live near a major airport because we fly so much.
- We needed to live in an area with good tennis facilities and access to good practice partners.
- We wanted to live in an area with great fishing. Very important.
- We desired to live in a suburban environment with a sizable Asian population. That wasn't the case in Henderson.

- We yearned to live in an area that had a reputation for being a great place to raise a family.
- We sought a place that was home to a good church.
- We wanted to live in an area with great natural beauty.

Beyond that, we were wide open. Well, maybe not so wide open. We weren't moving back to Minnesota. (No offense, my fellow Minnesotans, but I'm not into ice fishing and snowmobiling six months of the year.) Our criteria pointed us toward somewhere on the West Coast—and more north than south. San Francisco? Portland? Seattle?

Dad was the first one to suggest Seattle, and the more we discussed it over family mealtimes, the more we realized that Seattle fulfilled many of our criteria. The fact that Seattle was home to a sizable Asian community definitely was a plus for us.

"Well, when are we going to Seattle?" Carl asked. He was anxious to get going.

So was I. We all flew up to the Emerald City, and nature rolled out the red carpet: blue skies, warm temperatures, and a slight breeze. The first place we looked was Woodinville, a woodsy community about a half hour northeast of Seattle. Woodinville was like living in the . . . woods. We sure saw a lot of tall trees, and "downtown Woodinville" was populated by several mom-and-pop stores. You could run a herd of elk down Main Street on Saturday night and not worry about anyone getting hurt. We had grown accustomed to the suburbs—home to amenities such as supermarkets, Wal-Marts, and movie theaters. We also needed to be close to a good athletic club with indoor tennis courts.

Our real estate agent suggested a place called Medina, where saxophone artist Kenny G, the Nordstrom family, and some billionaire named Bill

Gates had built lavish custom homes. We took a look, and Medina wasn't our style. We huddled up. "Ah, where else could we live?" I asked the real estate agent.

"Well, there are many wonderful neighborhoods," was the reply. Over the next six months, we made several trips to Seattle to look over places such as Redmond, Issaquah, and Bellevue. We loved the lush greenery, the sparkling blue waterways filled with car-carrying ferryboats, and the coastline communities huddled around Lake Washington. Everywhere we gazed, we drew in beautiful shades of blue and green. Over that six-month span, we witnessed nothing but postcard views and sunny skies. A couple of people (okay, many people) mentioned that it does rain in Seattle, but that revelation didn't bother us. We were ready for a change from parched Henderson, and it had been a while since I had lived in a four-seasons environment. The only time we saw it rain in Seattle on our house-hunting excursions happened when we were overlooking Lake Washington in sun-filled skies. Suddenly, a light rain began to fall.

"Where is the rain coming from?" I asked. It was like a scene from a movie, where the sun is shining brightly while a beautiful summer shower drenches the two lovebirds. I surprisingly enjoyed this type of light rainfall where you could stand outside and not get soaked.

We began hearing more and more about a wonderful family-oriented community called Mercer Island, surrounded by Lake Washington and connected to Seattle to the west and Bellevue to the east by Interstate 90. Mercer Island, five miles long and two miles wide, had a reputation as a great place to raise a family. We asked questions about the schools, how many kids were on the island, and what type of recreation was available. I noted that Mercer Island was within twenty-five minutes of Sea-Tac, Seattle's international airport.

When we began looking at homes on Mercer Island, we initially asked to see houses not on the water. After several walk-throughs, Dad suggested, "Why don't you look at places on the lake?"

He didn't have to twist my arm. Once we walked through a certain ten-year-old house on the western coastline of Mercer Island, I fell in love with the home and the water. "This is where I want to live," I announced. Carl and Diana, who planned to live with me until they found their own place later, said it worked for them. The number of bedrooms, square footage, and lakeside view fit our criteria. The bonus was a dock, where I could tie up my boat when it wasn't in storage.

While Carl and I were Down Under for the Australian Open in January 1998, Diana remained behind to orchestrate the move from Henderson. I remember receiving an excited phone call from her shortly after the movers arrived.

"You wouldn't believe what happened today," she gushed. "This was the first time we've ever had anyone come over and bring us freshly baked cookies to welcome us into the neighborhood. Her name is Joyce Mark, and she was really friendly." Joyce eventually became such a good friend that we call her "Auntie Joyce."

I love my home and living on Mercer Island, and I'm looking forward to getting to know my neighbors better. When Diana became pregnant late in the summer of 1998, she and Carl began looking for a place of their own in earnest. Within a few months, they purchased a nice place about three minutes away by car. Mom and Dad's first grandchild, Katharine, was born June 4, 1999, and I love being an uncle.

There was an initial concern that moving to Seattle could hurt my tennis, but that's been no problem. Seattle, I discovered to my delight, has a reservoir of good practice partners to dip into—and someone always seems to be passing through. As for playing indoors, I had practiced inside bubble courts on many occasions back at the Green Valley Athletic Club in Henderson, so I could handle playing under a roof. Sometimes I booked courts at the Pro Sports Club or Mercer Island Country Club just a few minutes from home. I learned that being a professional tennis player, however, didn't cut it when it came to reserving a court in advance. After all, tennis is very popular in Seattle. If I called MICC a day or two before I wanted to play, I was often told that the only time available was 6 A.M. I don't mind getting up that early to go fishing, but not to play tennis!

WEDDING BELLS

As I mentioned, the move to Mercer Island was a move to the future, and it is my desire that my future includes marriage and raising a family. When I was in my teen years, I always thought I would be married by age twenty-three. I don't know why that age stuck out to me, but when I left high school and turned pro, I envisioned myself as a married man at the age of twenty-three.

Obviously, that did not happen. I have now turned the corner on thirty years of age, and I am still single. I don't question why God has not opened the door to marriage. Perhaps it is because He knows far better than me how difficult it would be on a marriage if I was concentrating on my tennis and traveling as much as I do. He knows the enormous responsibility of raising children and how important it would be for me *not* to be an absentee father. I know that God's timing is always perfect, so I'm trusting Him to work everything out.

Having said that, I very much desire to be married. I've seen firsthand how wonderful marriage can be in my parents' relationship and Carl and Diana's. Yet, I'm willing to wait, as this entry from my journal shows:

> August 17, 1998: This evening, I got a chance to spend some time by myself, and it was quite nice. I don't think I would want to do it every day, but to just have some peace and quiet occasionally is nice. I went to a baptism, and afterward I went out to eat at a Chinese restaurant all by myself. I was thinking that being single definitely has some good points and that maybe the Lord wants me to enjoy this time now because, indeed, most people spend more of their lives married and with someone than being single. I think this time is really good for me. I have lots of time to think, pray, and learn lots of things. I can take the time to better myself, too, which I am trying to do.

I've been involved in two serious dating relationships, but out of respect to those two young women, I'm not going to pour out my heart on my love life. I will make these general observations, however: the lifestyle I lead—always traveling and playing tennis—makes it difficult to get to know somebody. You always want to show your good side when you're dating, so it's hard to see what a person is really like and what his or her weaknesses are—and I include myself in this statement—when you blow into town for a few days between tournaments.

Then there is the desire to be discreet and not call attention to the relationship, out of fairness to her. I remember the time I was in Rome a few years back and an Italian journalist approached me in the players' lounge. "Hey, Michael," he said in a tone that I could tell was half serious, "how come Andre and Pete are dating these Hollywood starlets but you never seem to have one on your arm?"

I forced a laugh, but I would never want to have a public romance. And it's doubtful I would ever go out with a celebrity. But as I have matured over the years and grown in my Christian faith, I have learned that I want my future wife to have two distinctions:

1. *She needs to be of Chinese ancestry.* When I was in my teens and growing up in Southern California, it wasn't important for me to marry someone with a Chinese background. I was growing up in a melting pot of races and nationalities, and besides, Mom and Dad never said, "You *must* marry a Chinese."

After turning pro and making several trips to Asia, I learned that the Chinese culture is far bigger than little old me. My mentality has totally changed. I became prouder than ever that God made me Chinese. I feel a yearning to learn more about my heritage and pass it on to the next generation.

That's why I believe—unless the Lord makes it clear the other way—that I will eventually marry someone of Chinese descent, probably a Chinese-American.

2. *She needs to be a Christian.* The Bible is very clear on this: we are not to be "unequally yoked" when it comes to marriage. "Do not be yoked together with unbelievers," instructs the apostle Paul in 2 Corinthians 6:14. God wants the Christian believer to always have Him as his first love, and if I cannot share my first and greatest love with my spouse, then something is not right. On top of all this, you want to be of the same mind and the same wavelength on spiritual matters with your mate.

I know the Lord has a special person waiting for me, and I am willing to wait for her in more ways than one. Allow me to explain further. When I was sixteen years old, I gave an interview to *Sports Illustrated* in which I made a rather bold statement that I would wait until marriage to have sex.

I have kept that promise to myself and to my future wife.

I realize that some of you reading the previous sentence may choose not to believe me, but it's true. You may say that it's impossible, but all things are possible with God's help. You may not understand why I have chosen not to have sex, but I understand very well.

The Bible is clear on this point: sex is reserved for married couples. My parents raised me with a certain perspective on how special marriage is and how important sexual purity should be. I can recall the times when Mom would drive me to school, and during those fifteen minutes when she had a captive audience, she would say, "Michael, if you have any questions about drugs or drinking or even sex, we can talk about it."

And we did. That's how Mom was. She was very open about sex— even blunt about the topic. She never sat me down and gave me a list of dos and don'ts. Instead, she and Dad waited for those teachable moments to impart their wisdom about sexual purity.

They told me that it's worth it to save sex for marriage and keep myself pure for the woman God wants me to spend my life with. They reminded me that the Lord designed sex that way for a good reason and that plenty of people who disregarded His plan would tell me how much they regretted giving their virginity away. You see, I'm looking forward to that wedding night when I can give my wife something that I have not shared with anyone else in the whole wide world.

Oh, I've faced pressure, from guys on the tour and acquaintances, to compromise my values. Tennis has its share of "groupies"—young women who pop up at tour events and make it known that they are willing and able to spend the night with the celebrity pros. Yes, the opportunities are there, but I purposely chose not to put myself in situations where it would be easy to yield to sexual temptation.

Something that has stuck with me is the famous "love chapter" in the Bible—1 Corinthians 13, where love is described as being patient, kind, not envious, not boastful, not proud, and not self-seeking. That first definition caught my attention. The fact that love should be patient has always stuck with me in the context of sex. If you really love somebody, then you should be willing to wait to share something like that.

Besides showing patience, there is the respect factor. I have always kept this thought in the back of mind when I've dated someone: treat her in the same way I hope that some other guy is treating my future wife.

A CLOSING THOUGHT

I would like to close this chapter by addressing the teens and young adults reading this book. You may be blown away to learn that I am a virgin and will remain so until my wedding night. Or maybe you are pleasantly surprised. Either way, I would like to encourage you to wait as well. It's worth it to make that commitment—even if you are the only one among your friends or colleagues who is willing to wait to have sex. Just remember who you are. You will protect yourself from a variety of sexually transmitted diseases. You will protect yourself from the possibility of becoming a parent before you are mature enough or financially able to support and raise that child. And you will protect your mind from making sexual comparisons when and if you do marry.

But Michael, I'm already sexually experienced.

Yes, you've jumped the gun, but you can commit yourself to God to remain pure until your wedding day and become what is called a "renewed virgin." You see, teens and young people who have fallen short can become virgins again in the sight of God. Once you confess your sin and admit your desire for God's forgiveness, it is as though you never had sex with that partner (or partners). The Lord tells us in Isaiah 43:25 that "I, even I, am he who blots out your transgressions, for my own sake, and remembers your sins no more."

Isn't that a great promise? You can depend on God to keep His word.

• CARL AND ME FISHING FOR CHINOOK
SALMON AT HOH RIVER •

•

CHAPTER 10

FISHER OF MEN

I'm hooked on fishing, and I have been for a long time. In fact, I've been fishing longer than I've been playing tennis. Dad first put a fishing pole in my hands when I was probably four years old and living in Minnesota. I think Dad got interested in the pastime because fishing and hunting are practically state religions in the Land of 10,000 Lakes. With a tackle shop on every street corner, fishing and hunting are what people talk about.

During the warm summer months, Dad and Mom took Carl and me fishing nearly every weekend at a place we called Power Plant because the fishing spot was located on the Saint Croix River near a large power plant. Mom would pack a lunch and make bait by mixing corn, dough, and cotton—inexpensive bait, to be sure, but effective. Although the Saint Croix River was wide enough for people to troll from boats, we always fished from the shoreline, probably because it was cheaper that way. Carl and I didn't mind. We giggled when, out of the blue, the fish would jump out of the water, some so close to the shore they landed on the dirt. Dog pile! Carl and I dove to see who could get to the flapping fish first and toss it into our bucket.

Power Plant was home to carp, silver bass, and freshwater croakers, and there was nothing better than catching a baker's dozen and having a fish fry on Saturday night. Mom prepared different Chinese dishes with our catches, and my mouth still waters as I recall Carl and I filling our tummies with these delicious fish caught by our own hands. Fishing became so much fun that all it took was for one of my parents to say, "Let's go fishing," and Carl and I would hightail it to the garage to get our rods ready while Mom packed a lunch and patted together her homemade bait.

We fished into fall, but when Minnesota froze over in the wintertime, ice fishing in sub-zero temperatures was *too* cold. I remember Dad taking us out a couple of times to a frozen lake, where someone with a big drill popped a hole in the ice for us. Carl and I, bundled with every layer of clothing that we owned, baited our hooks and dipped a line into the frozen mush, but after a half hour of standing over the hole and turning frostbite-blue from exposure, we packed it in. We loved fishing, but not enough to freeze while doing it.

Later, when we moved to the warmer climate of California, fishing became more than a hobby—it became a passion. As I said in chapter 4, Carl and I loved our predawn fishing expeditions to the La Costa golf resort, but we also fished San Marcos Creek, which flowed into La Costa. Located in the brushlands of Box Canyon, San Marcos Creek was pocketed with small ponds filled with bass and crawdads. Then Dad introduced us to sea fishing on half-day boats leaving the San Diego harbor. Fishing became a fun way to relax and have fun—the perfect antidote to the high-pressure world of junior tennis and climbing up in the rankings. What other sport allows you to get outside and enjoy nature, relax while working a line, visit with family and friends, and still mix in a little excitement and challenge? The answer, for me, was fishing.

When I reached my early teen years, I thought it would be great to become a marine biologist so I could study fish and work with them. I did school reports on fish, asked Dad to take me to sporting goods stores, and fished year-round at nearby reservoirs stocked with trout and catfish. Then I wanted to bring live fish *into* the home. When we moved from La Costa to Placentia following my ninth-grade year, I asked Mom and Dad if I could get an aquarium. A friend had told me that African cichlids were great fish to have around because they came in so many bright, colorful varieties. My first tank was twenty-nine gallons.

After suffering that hip injury at the end of the 1989 season, I had some idle time on my hands. Let's go buy more aquariums! Mom let me take up a chunk of the living room with a 180-gallon aquarium, which I filled with more African cichlids. My aquarium-and-African-cichlid buying spree was not over, however. Within a few months, I had five freshwater aquariums in the house.

I'm not sure that's why we *had* to move from Placentia to a bigger home in Coto de Caza in 1990, but it could have been because we were running out of room for all my aquariums. My parents suggested using one of the garages at the new house to store all my tanks—they put their foot down and said no aquariums inside the home. At one time, I had at least twenty-five freshwater aquariums on the property, ranging from ten gallons to three hundred gallons. They were filled with fifteen different species of African cichlids, varying in size from less than two inches to twelve inches long. My most prized fish was the *Cyphotilapia frontosa;* one of those sixteen-inch puppies set me back one hundred dollars. Most of my everyday, run-of-the-mill African cichlids, however, cost me anywhere from two to ten bucks a fish.

So why am I so interested in these small freshwater creatures from the African continent? African cichlids, some of the most colorful fish in the world, come in different shapes and sizes from various lakes in Africa: Lake Malawi, Lake Tanganyika, and the famous Lake Victoria. Believe it or not, African cichlids have different personalities. You can tell whether they are in different moods by their colors and how they move in the water.

African cichlids are territorial; when I put little plaster houses in the aquarium and other fish happen to enter them, the cichlids chase them out. I found that I'd better not put more than seven big African cichlids in one aquarium unless I want to watch a fish fight.

The way the males court the females is interesting: the males turn vibrant colors as they dance around the females in a courting manner. When the females spawn, they incubate the eggs inside their mouths to keep them circulating.

All those eggs eventually turn into little fish, so I trade in my extra African cichlids at the pet store for credit. Cichlids are highly collectible fish, but I don't buy mine from pet stores. I prefer to purchase mine from collectors around the world. I deal with an African cichlid breeder from Hanover, Germany, along with a fellow from New Jersey. I've discovered a whole network of African cichlid wholesalers out there.

FISHING FOR STRIPERS

Watching fish is amusing, but fishing for them is tons more fun. When Carl and I moved to Nevada in 1991, having Lake Mead in our backyard was certainly a big lure. Our home was a twenty-five-minute drive from the

huge reservoir behind Hoover Dam, so I purchased a Ranger bass boat—
my first big toy! Carl and I would tow it to Lake Mead each time we went
fishing, which happened to be almost any time that we were in Henderson
for longer than a two-day shot. My Ranger could fit up to seven people. I
had a lot of goodies on my boat as well: a trolling motor, fish finders, locker
storage space, and a CD player and speakers.

Lake Mead's calling card was striped bass, but the lake only seemed to
yield a couple of stripers each time Carl and I visited. That development
frustrated me and caused Carl to lose interest.

"Come on, Carl. Let's go fishing," I said one December day during our
annual break.

"Nah, there's never any fish in there," he whined. "Every time we go to
Mead, we're lucky if we catch one or two little ones. It's a waste of time."

"But you have to find a pattern to find out where they are," I pointed
out. "Just give me some time, and I'll figure it out."

I had a fish finder on my boat, a high-tech device similar to a sonar
unit that told me what was underneath the boat. I could see fish on the
screen. I would "mark" them, but when we cast our lines, no nibbles.

Carl remained unconvinced. Then I had an idea: Why not hire a fishing
guide? That was the answer. Besides showing us where to find fish, our guide
also taught us different fishing techniques and "presentations." A presentation is hard to describe, but is something you change depending on the time
of the year. The last time Carl and I went out on Lake Mead, we caught lots
of stripers, all ranging between two and five pounds. Now, whenever we
return to Lake Mead on vacation, we hire a guide and go for the gusto.

I sold my Ranger bass boat when we moved from Henderson to
Mercer Island, replacing it with a bigger and deeper white-and-red
Ranger 620VS Fisherman. I was in seventh heaven having a great lake

and a dock in my front yard. Now I could go fishing any time I wanted, in the early morning hours when the world is calm or in the middle of the night when jet leg wakes me up.

Lake Washington is a *huge* body of water with plenty of room for fishermen and jet skiers. From what I've seen, there is not much fishing pressure on Lake Washington. I think the locals prefer to try their luck in countless other lakes in the Seattle area. One of them is Lake Sammamish, which is one of the most-recognized smallmouth bass fisheries in the nation. I've fished at Lake Sammamish, but most of my fishing is near my home on Lake Washington; I have a couple of secret spots that took some time to find. The biggest smallmouth bass I've been able to land has been close to six pounds. I have tried fishing in the Puget Sound, where I've caught sand dabs (which look like small flounders) and a few Chinook salmon, the biggest being around eight pounds. I've even pulled in a few dogfish, but I'm trying not to brag.

The move to Washington state necessitated a change in my fishing mentality—no longer were we fishing in the calm waters behind Hoover Dam but in the bustling waters of Lake Washington and Puget Sound. The sound isn't as bumpy as the open seas, but I prefer fishing in quiet freshwater lakes and waterways to the rolling, open sea because I've always had trouble with seasickness. It's ironic—I love to fish, but I have to deal with seasickness!

Fishing in the Pacific Northwest also necessitated equipment changes. Instead of pursuing striped bass at Lake Mead, I needed to purchase the correct rods, reels, and lures to go after smallmouth bass. After several shopping trips, Mom said I should open up a fishing tackle shop out of my garage. She's probably right. I don't indulge myself with material possessions, but I do get a little light-headed when I walk into a well-stocked tackle shop or fishing store.

Fishing and Tennis

I found fishing, in some ways, to be similar to tennis. Preparation and technique were important, as well as planning how you were going to beat that fish. That meant you had to choose the right hook, position the boat just so, pick the right lure—plastic worms, spinnerbaits, crankbaits, or surface plugs—or choose the correct live bait, such as night crawlers, crayfish, mealworms, or water dogs.

I tried to indulge in my passion whenever I was on the road, although that was not as simple as it sounds. Sometimes my on-the-road fishing expeditions were as simple as tossing a line into the ponds around the golf greens at PGA West in Indian Wells. Other times, we would drive to some small fishing hole, like Swan Lake in Cincinnati, where I foul-hooked an eight-pound carp.

The best tennis tournament for fishing has turned out to be the Lipton (now known as the Ericsson Open) in Miami each March. I have chartered boats after early-round losses to fish for mahi-mahi and sailfish, or maybe hook into some snapper and barracuda. Loads of fun.

One year I traveled to Boca Raton to do an appearance for Prince rackets, so they chartered a boat for everyone in our party. I hauled in a forty-five-pound amberjack, which put up a nice fight before we landed it. I had to show *everybody* this beautiful fish that I caught when we returned. Then I was surprised a couple of hours later at a luncheon hosted by Prince when my amberjack was part of the meal! To answer the question in your mind: yes, I like to eat all kinds of fish. If Mom is preparing it, she usually steams and spices the fish Chinese style. I also love sushi and sashimi.

Fishing in Europe has been a nonstarter for me. I haven't found fishing to be much fun over there. Maybe it's because they practice what I call "still fishing." You just stand by the bank of a listless stream and let the line sit in the water. Too still for me—it's like watching grass grow. I prefer the action of lure fishing from a slow-moving boat.

Over the years, I've had some great fishing experiences. Let me tell you about a few that stand out in my mind:

- Following an early-round loss at Wimbledon in 1996, the whole family and I flew to Juneau, Alaska, where we boarded a boat that took us to a beautiful fishing lodge along the Alaskan coast. The goal was to fish for king salmon, but we were a little late for that season. Instead, we caught much silver salmon, pink salmon, halibut, and rock cod. One day we went upstream and caught Dolly Vardens, a type of fish. We brought back eight four-foot-long boxes of frozen fish. We and everyone we knew feasted for months.

- In early 2000, Carl, Dad, and I stopped in New Zealand after the Australian campaign for several days of fishing in that picturesque country. We drove from Auckland to the Bay of Islands, where we chartered a boat and tried to catch some marlin. We were unsuccessful, although we did land some yellowtail tuna, which the Kiwis call a kingfish.

- Cabo San Lucas, at the very tip of Baja, California, was our port of call for a fishing trip with family and a few friends in December 1994. We landed some striped marlin, but they were not trophy size.

- Finally, I'll never forget the fishing trip/bachelor's party that I threw for Carl prior to his wedding to Diana in 1995. I booked a charter boat out of San Diego for Carl and eighteen friends and cousins to go catch yellowfin. We found yellowfin, all right. We hauled in more than a ton of fish, which the deck crew either fil-leted or left whole. We were allowed to keep five fish per person, and each fish weighed between twenty-five and forty-five pounds.

My poor cousin Jimmy. When we arrived back at the dock, we unloaded a half dozen black Hefty bags filled with fresh fish. We stacked those bags of yellowfin in the back of his minivan, not noticing that the bags were leaking fish blood. It took us an hour to get back to Orange County, and by that time, Jimmy's van reeked with the smell of fish guts.

The following evening, we invited all our friends and feasted on tuna steaks, tuna salad, and tuna sushi. Anyway you could have tuna, we had it. I felt sorry for Jimmy, though. Even after thoroughly washing out his van and wiping up fish blood, the rancid smell stayed in the van for weeks. But we sure had a great bachelor's party!

FINAL FISHING THOUGHT

I have named my nineteen-foot walleye bass boat "Fisher of Men" for a particular reason. It is an apt name for my boat because it has been my great hope that my tennis career—playing before thousands in person and millions on TV—has helped me be a "fisher of men." If I have been able to draw people to the Lord through my tennis, then the fame and the money and the rankings won't compare to touching people's lives and encouraging them in the Lord, because that's something that lasts a life-time and beyond.

There's a great bumper sticker out there that sums up the whole fish-ing experience for me:

Be ye fishers of men. You catch 'em—He'll clean 'em.

Courtesy of the Chang Family

• APPLAUSE FROM PRINCESS DIANA AT THE AWARD
CEREMONY AT THE SALEM OPEN IN HONG KONG •

———— • ————

CHAPTER II

YEARS OF REFINEMENT

Remember how at the end of chapter 8 I said things got worse before they got better after my disastrous 1998? Well, they got *a lot* worse. Overnight, players I had handled easily in the past were licking their chops when they saw that we had been paired against each other in the draw. They played with greater confidence, I played with ebbing confidence, and the result was early exits for me. Midway through the year, I got past the second round in only one of fourteen tournaments.

As I began to doubt my ability to come through on the big points, I also ran into spiritual doubts. In my journal, I wrote: *Lord, what have I done wrong? Haven't I been faithful? Haven't I been following You?*

I remember hearing a pastor say one time that whenever he goes somewhere to preach and immediately encounters obstacles, then he knows that God wants him to be there. I was where God wanted me to be, but I was facing a mound of obstacles. I finally reached a point where I said to myself, "You know, I could spend all my time trying to understand, but it still won't change anything." I decided to seek refuge on the practice court, but the harder I tried to improve my game, the worse I played.

One event brightened my attitude. After I lost early at the French Open, I returned to Mercer Island because Carl and Diana were about to become parents for the first time. While Diana was at Overlake Hospital in Bellevue, my mother and I went shopping for diapers and baby clothes. Mom was pretty excited at the prospect of becoming a grandmother. Then I received a phone call from Carl on my cell phone.

"The baby's out!" said my frantic brother.

"What?" I asked. "You were supposed to call when it looked like she was going to deliver."

"The baby's out!" It soon became obvious that Carl was too excited to say anything else.

We dropped our shopping plans and rushed over to Overlake Hospital, where we greeted Katharine Jie-An Chang into the world on June 4, 1999.

The Chinese believe it is important for nursing moms to eat striped bass because the fish contains important nutrients and minerals that infants need in their mother's milk. For the next month, Mom shopped for striped bass at a nearby Chinese market, using her expertise in the kitchen to prepare the fish in different ways for Diana. That is the kind of love Mom has for the family.

A CHALLENGING EVENT

When Andre Agassi fell off the radar screen in 1997 and plummeted to No. 141, he started his comeback by playing a Challenger event in

Burbank, a Los Angeles suburb. Although my ranking wasn't in the triple digits, I needed to win some matches, so in July, I dropped down into the Challenger circuit. I didn't have to travel to Singapore or practice with fuzzless balls as Carl had, but I did enter a Challenger event in Aptos in the San Francisco Bay Area. While children played in a sandbox behind my court, I had more adult things to worry about—such as trying to beat my opponent. I did win three rounds, but I was stopped in the semifinals by Harel Levy, a twenty-year-old Israeli player ranked No. 241 in the world.

Later that month I returned to Southern California to play the Los Angeles event. I won a couple of matches to reach the quarterfinals against a qualifier named James Sekulov. I cruised 6–2 in the first set, but I felt I was playing horribly. I kept putting pressure on myself to put this unheralded player away. At 1–2 on serve in the second set, I missed an easy forehand, and I mentally lost it. I slapped my thigh and bellowed, "How could I miss that shot?"

Throughout the rest of the match, I asked myself that question with regularity. I played myself out of a winning game and snapped defeat from the jaws of victory, losing the next two sets, 6–2, 6–2.

After the match, I was reeling in the locker room. Really frustrated. Dad and Carl stayed with me for moral support.

"I can't believe I played that bad a match," I stewed. "I'm at the point where I don't want to play anymore."

Dad and Carl said nothing. They let me vent.

"I'm done," I said. "That's it. I don't want to play anymore."

"Michael," said my father. "You're frustrated. That's why you're saying those things. There's always tomorrow."

I looked up and stared at him. I did not know what I wanted to do, but I knew that if I was going to give matches away like this one, I didn't want to play tennis anymore.

I took a few days off to gain some perspective. I wasn't going to quit, so I didn't raise the subject again. I had Cincinnati coming up, the U.S. Open . . . and then my fall swing through Asia. I continued to perform poorly, however, including a second-round loss at Flushing Meadow to Arnaud Clement of France. Now I had to drag my weary mind and body to Shanghai.

Mom had been talking to my Uncle I-ping about my tennis, asking him what she could say to encourage me. Mom and I are very close, and we talk about these things.

"Michael, I know you are going through a hard time, and that you aren't very happy."

"That's right, Mommy."

"You have to make the effort to get yourself out of this," she said.

"I know, but I'm trying."

"I'm not talking about your tennis," said Mom. "I'm talking about your spirit. You have to lift yourself up."

What Mom was saying was that only I had the power to change my perspective on life and on tennis, and she was right.

I flew to Shanghai, a long haul to be sure. In my hotel room on the eve of my first match, I noticed my *Life Application Bible* on the nightstand, where I always put it when I travel. I lay down on my bed and opened up my Bible, where half the page is Scripture and the other half is filled with notes and commentary explaining what the verses say or what God is trying to teach His people. As I began reading, a deep, emotional feeling grew in my heart. I came to a point of brokenness, and tears streamed down my face. "Lord, I just don't have any joy in my life," I cried. "I'm tired of trying, period. I'm going to give my tennis career completely to You." I had made that statement to God before, but I think I always hung on to a little piece of my tennis. Now I was at the point of complete brokenness.

That evening was a big turning point for me. It is often said that God can't do anything with you until He has broken you to the point where He can rebuild you. That's what He did with me. I had been holding on for so long. Trying too hard. And now I was going to relinquish it all to Him.

INTO THE QUALIES

I would love to be able to write that I surprised the tennis world by capturing a second Grand Slam title after everyone had written me off, but that hasn't happened since that emotional moment in Shanghai.

Since my ranking stood at No. 78, that meant I didn't qualify for the top-tier events. In late November, I wanted to play the last tournament of the year—the Paris Indoors. I asked my agent, Tom Ross of Octagon, to inquire about receiving a wild card, but he was told that nothing could be done for me.

So I entered the qualification tournament, something I hadn't done since I was fifteen years old, and played my way into the tournament. My confidence building with each match, I advanced all the way to the semifinals before losing a close three-setter to Marat Safin. This gave me a year-end ranking of No. 50.

In Paris, I heard The Question I had begun hearing during the summer season: "So, Michael, when are you going to retire?"

At first, I was annoyed. *Hey, wait a minute! Just because I lost a few matches, now you want to retire me!* I was only twenty-seven years old and just two years from the top 5, and now the press was poised to write my tennis obituary. After the initial shock, I began to understand where the press was coming from. I was losing to players to whom I had never lost, and I was struggling to stay in tournaments beyond the second round. When you don't win, it is natural to hear some scribe shout out from the back of the pressroom, "Well, Michael, is this going to be your last year?"

My standard answer became this: "I haven't thought much about it. Things have obviously been difficult, but we all have our ups and downs." Another reason it was difficult to answer that question was the way that pro tennis is staged. We, the players, are independent contractors, which means that we do not have managers or head coaches pacing the dugout or sidelines determining our fate. No one ever says, "Hey, Chang! Coach wants to see you, and be sure to bring your playbook."

Since I was just twenty-seven years old, I believed I still had plenty of good tennis left in me. After my horrible 1999 season, the new millennium turned out to be better. In January 2000, I played my way into the final of Auckland in New Zealand, reached the semis of four tournaments (including two grass court tournaments leading up to Wimbledon), and won Los Angeles! The irony of winning in my old hometown, before my parents and my relatives from Thousand Oaks—after I wanted to chuck my rackets into the Pacific Ocean just a year earlier—caused my voice to break several times when I gave my victory speech at the UCLA Tennis Center. I was wrought with emotion because I had wondered if I would ever win another ATP tournament again.

The unexpected win in Los Angeles vaulted me back into the top 30, and I could breathe easier again. In tournament after tournament, I expected another renaissance, but that never happened. A combination of some dismal tennis and tough draws produced a dry gulch as far as mining points during the 2001 season.

There were a couple of memorable experiences, however, and one was being involved with China's bid to host the 2008 Summer Olympics. A week before Wimbledon and several weeks before the International Olympic Committee met in Moscow to vote, I participated in a press conference in London announcing my support and my volunteer role to bring the Olympics to the world's most populous country for the first time.

I noted that China had changed significantly while believing it would open up further if awarded the right to host the Summer Games. "If China becomes the host nation, I think you're going to see something very, very special," I said in London. "The Chinese know that this is an opportunity that doesn't come around very often. They know how precious this is. For the first Olympics in China, they're going to want to make this the best ever."

China won the 2008 bid, and now I'm looking forward to seeing what happens in the intervening years. I'm truly optimistic that hosting the Olympics will serve as a catalyst to further positive change in China. Only time will tell.

• COOKING A THANKSGIVING MEAL •

—— • ——

CHAPTER 12

GIVING TO OTHERS

O ne afternoon, I was strolling through Target with Mom. I forget what we were shopping for, but we stopped to look over some merchandise. Just beyond my peripheral vision, I could see two teenage boys glancing my way. After years in the public eye, you get a sixth sense for when someone is watching you.

One boy leaned close to his friend and whispered, "Hey, that's Michael Chang. I'm sure it's him."

They couldn't tell that I could overhear every word. While I minded my own business, the other fellow sneaked a look at me. A quick glance was all he needed. "Are you kidding?" he said to his friend. "Do you really think Michael Chang shops at Target?"

They didn't notice my soft chuckle, but then I thought, *What's wrong with shopping at Target?* Maybe it's the celebrity culture we live in, but I found it interesting that some people cannot grasp that I do ordinary things—or *like* to do ordinary things. Besides shopping at Target, I fill my car with gas, stand in line at the bank, and buy my own tennis balls at Costco.

Yes, I shop for tennis balls at Costco, one of those cavernous, stack-it-to-the-ceiling warehouse clubs where you can buy forty-eight rolls of toilet paper, five-pound tubs of peanut butter, and ninety-six frozen tacquitos. Since I like to shave a few bucks just as much as the next person, I purchase my Penn tennis balls in bulk when I make one of my shopping forays to Costco. I fill my basket with four to six boxes of Penn balls: each box, which costs $23.79, holds twelve cans. I admit that I have received some interesting looks when pushing my big cart filled with tennis balls through a crowded Costco—kind of like Julia Child dropping four sacks of twenty-five-pound bags of flour into a shopping basket or NASCAR driver Jeff Gordon purchasing a set of four tires there.

"Gosh, you have to buy your *own* balls?" is the typical response from the young woman checking me out.

"Yup, I'm afraid I do," I replied.

"But aren't you sponsored for those?"

"Well, tennis ball companies don't sponsor anybody. They hardly make any money on their balls anyway because they sell them so cheap. They just want to get people playing the game."

"Oh. Sure seems funny to me."

Four boxes or forty-eight cans of Penn balls don't last very long around the Chang household—about a week when I'm in town. It takes two boxes to fill a small basket, and then I'm always popping open new cans when I play practice sets. It is part of the cost of being a professional tennis player.

Remember how I told you about Mom's frugality when she had to stretch every dollar in our junior days? I've never forgotten the financial sacrifices she and my father made for Carl and me—or my roots. I was raised in a middle-class family, and while the Lord has blessed me financially beyond my wildest dreams, I'm glad my parents taught me the value of a dollar and of living conservatively and within my means. Those are values I want to instill in my children someday.

I like hunting for good deals and shopping around for the best price, especially for my fishing gear. Believe me, I know when the Bass Pro Shop in Springfield, Missouri, which sells mostly fishing and hunting gear, has its periodical sales. If I can save ten bucks on a certain item, I'll take it. I love to participate in their "cash points back" program that rewards frequent shoppers.

Spending money wisely is the reason I fly coach in the United States—even if I'm flying coast-to-coast. As someone once told me, the first-class passengers arrive less than a second faster than those sitting in the peanut-and-pretzel seats in the back. Seriously, I can't justify paying thousands of dollars more for a flight from Seattle to Atlanta, for instance, for the privilege of sitting in a leather seat in first class. Having said that, I can justify flying in business class on long-haul flights to Europe and Asia. Fourteen to sixteen hours scrunched up in a coach seat are a lot different from a four-hour hop—and a lot harder on my body.

The reason I'm telling you this is because I am careful with the way I spend money. The Bible has more to say about money than any other subject, and I take very seriously God's direction that we support His church and His work. God's Word says in 2 Corinthians 9:6 that whoever sows sparingly will reap sparingly, and whoever sows generously will reap generously. A verse later, it tells us that "each man should give what he has decided in his heart to give, not reluctantly or under compulsion, for God loves a cheerful giver." That's why I, along with my parents and Carl and Diana, have started the Chang Family Foundation, a nonprofit foundation funded by our charitable gifts. We want to sow generously and give cheerfully.

Nonetheless, I also try to follow the biblical admonition from Matthew 6:2–4: "So when you give to the needy, do not announce it with trumpets, as the hypocrites do in the synagogues and on the streets, to be honored by men. I tell you the truth, they have received their reward in full. But when you give to the needy, do not let your left hand know what your right hand is doing, so that your giving may be in secret. Then your Father, who sees what is done in secret, will reward you." These verses explain why I am reluctant to write in further detail about my financial giving to God's work, but it is something that I believe is important for every Christian. The reason we created the foundation—another one of Carl's ideas—is because we have been so blessed as a family, and we want to share the resources that God has poured forth our way.

THE NEXT GENERATION CAMPS

The Chang Family Foundation was started in 1999 with a mission to introduce the good news of Jesus Christ to the world through local and international youth programs, and to grow and nurture young people in their personal relationship with God. One of the first things we did was hold our first NeXt Generation Tennis Camp in the summer of 2000 at Industry Hills, a suburb north of Orange County and east of Los Angeles. The nearly weeklong event was billed as a Christian outreach tennis camp, and we were able to find enough Christian counselors and coaches to keep our on-court ratio at 5:1. We felt that we could impact the kids most by keeping the groups small. I think we had twenty-five kids that week. We paid for scholarships for those who couldn't afford the modest registration fee.

I rotated from court to court, playing with the young students, doing drills with them, and even playing "Around the World," a silly game in which you hit the ball over the net and then have to run over to the other side and get in line. (I won, beating Carl in the finals.) Many, if not all, of the juniors were ranked in Southern California, so we formed teams for some intramural competition.

I remember reaching the finals of the team competition with a junior named Walter. We were playing best-of-three tiebreakers against Cami Benjamin (who used to play on the women's pro tour) and her partner, and it went to the final point of the third tiebreaker before we lost. Sorry about that, Walter!

After a long day of running and playing tennis, we showered and ate dinner at a nearby hotel. We lined up great youth speakers who talked about what it means to live a life devoted to Christ. For our Thursday "At the Net" night program, we had over seven hundred people show up, and more than two dozen people decided to become Christians that night or rededicate their lives to Christ.

An evening program would not be complete without having a little fun—at my expense. The counselors put on a few skits, including one with a David Letterman–like list for the "Top Ten Real Ways You Can Tell Michael Chang Is Playing."

"Number ten. Look to see if he is wearing tight shorts."

"Number nine. Does he have a bowl haircut?"

You get the idea.

We followed up Industry Hills by having our second outreach tennis camp in Taipei, Taiwan, following the 2001 Australian Open. We worked with various Christian organizations in Taiwan and had around sixty kids show up—just the right number. We learned that it takes a lot of manpower to put on a camp, and finding good counselors, coaches, volunteers, and excellent staff can make or break the week, because Carl and I can't be everywhere.

The NeXt Generation camps are something we hope to continue in coming years, both in the U.S. and overseas. We haven't forgotten how it felt not to have opportunities to play tournaments or get coaching. If we can help youngsters excel in their talent, at a cost they can afford, then the camps are successful. I like working with kids because of their simplicity and innocence, and their attitudes and gifts.

In addition, we will be holding local Christian sports leagues and working with several churches to reach out to friends and family members who may not know Jesus. The Foundation has partnered with like-minded organizations that have a desire to bring people to Christ. If you would like more information about how you can partner with the Foundation or participate in future events, please contact Caroline Ko, our wonderful program director at our office in Bellevue, Washington. Here is how you can reach us:

The Chang Family Foundation
Caroline Ko
14150 N.E. 20th Street PMB 233
Bellevue, WA 98007
(425) 373-1400
e-mail: cffoundation@mchang.com

Much is in the works for the future of the Chang Family Foundation, and I'm sure I will be devoting more time and attention to the Foundation after I leave professional tennis. So far, it has been rewarding to work with people who have such a heart for the Lord, on top of seeing lives changed in God's own unique way. It is also exciting to think about what the Lord has in store.

CHAPTER 13

FAQs—Frequently Asked Questions

I like being interviewed, which is fortunate because I've answered many questions put my way over the years. Now my writing partner, Mike Yorkey, has me in the interview room. Here's a transcript of our little press conference:

Why were you never called Mike Chang?

If you knew me before eighth grade, then you called me Mike. I think my parents insisted on me being called Michael at that time because I was named after my grandfather Michael Tung, who was always called Michael. I'm glad my parents stuck to their guns. "Michael Chang" also has a more melodious sound to it than the more abrupt "Mike Chang."

Can the top juniors make it to the pros today without going to a tennis academy?

It's rare to see a young player coming up who hasn't gone the academy route, but I still believe there's a place for a "home grown" player like myself. I would think that living in a tennis-rich area like California, Texas, or Florida would help young players get the competition they need to improve their games.

You and Pete Sampras were obviously good friends in your junior days, but what happened to that friendship after you won Roland Garros?

In the fall of 1988, Franz Lidz of *Sports Illustrated* wanted to do a story about me, so one afternoon, Mom, Pete, and I went fishing with Franz on Saguaro Lake outside Phoenix. For a couple of hours, Pete was a captive audience as he listened to me talk about myself with the *SI* reporter. Then he was identified in the story as "Michael's sometime doubles partner."

After I won the French, I'm certain that Pete didn't want other people to typecast him as "Michael's sometime doubles partner." Of course, I never felt that way about Pete. As far I was concerned, Pete was Pete, and I knew he would be a great player one day.

Still, Pete had ambitions of his own, so he made a break during the summer of 1989. *Break* might be too harsh a word—I think we drifted apart and went our separate ways. Having said that, we have remained friends over the years although we never hung out together after the early years. That's understandable, as it's difficult to remain very close when you're competing at such a high level.

I know that each of us has respected what the other has accomplished. For years to come, tennis historians and fans will debate whether Pete was the greatest player ever, and he certainly can make that claim since he has won more Grand Slams than any other male player.

How do you deal with all the travel and living out of a suitcase?

Certainly, the road life is one of the most difficult aspects about being a professional tennis player. One way I cope is by trying to maintain my privacy when I shut my hotel door. Many times during my career, my parents or Carl have gone out, found Chinese takeout, and brought it back to the hotel room to share with me. Too many fans—some well meaning and some not—interrupted our restaurant meals to have a word or ask for an autograph. It was hard to relax and enjoy my food in that kind of atmosphere.

Privacy has always been important to me, which is why I constantly set out the "Do Not Disturb" sign. Otherwise, I have maids and hotel employees knocking on my door to restock the minibar, turn down my pillow, or see if there is anything I need. Sometimes they knock, wait two seconds, and open the door—while I'm stepping out of the shower.

I try to make my room my little home away from home. Cleanliness may be next to godliness, although not all my fellow pros feel that way—which reminds me of a funny story about a player on tour. It seems that this player went out to practice, and upon his return to the hotel, the manager met him in the lobby.

"Excuse me, but we have some bad news," said the manager.

The player was stunned. "What happened?"

"When the maid went into your room, she found that your room had been robbed. We sincerely apologize for this event, and we want to try to help."

"Oh, no," moaned the player. "What did they get?"

"We're still trying to determine that," said the manager. "Shall we go take a look at your room?"

When the manager flung open the door, the player's jaw dropped.

"Nope, that's just the way I left it," said the player. He hadn't been robbed at all. He had just left a messy room!

As for me, I've learned to live out of a suitcase over the years. I pack twelve to fifteen playing shirts, a dozen pairs of shorts, twenty pairs of socks, a couple of warm-up suits, some jeans and dress clothes, and shoes—including three to six pairs of tennis shoes, which usually last me about a couple of weeks. (I usually have more Reebok shoes waiting for me at the tournament site, if needed.)

I have learned a few tricks on the road. When you fly from one city to another in Europe, they weigh your luggage and try to sock you with some serious "overweight" charges. Since the weight rules for international flights are more generous than intra-Europe flights, I have to point out that my ticket is part of an *international* ticket because I started my trip in the States. We've saved ourselves a bundle over the years by taking advantage of this rule.

How do you go to church when you're on tour?

It's hard to go to church when I'm playing tournaments. The finals are always scheduled on Sunday, or Sunday becomes a travel day. But when it works out, I enjoy visiting new churches or returning to the ones I've been to before. Whether or not I'm able to get to church when I travel, I read my Bible and pray and communicate with God daily. Some of my closest times with God have happened on the road because I've had to lean on Him for support.

When I'm back at Mercer Island, my home church is The Lighthouse, an Asian-American church in Factoria. The pastor, Wayne Ogimachi, is the same pastor that my sister-in-law Diana had when she was attending the University of California at Berkeley, so there's a lot of history there. I like their mix of music as well. Prior to attending the Lighthouse, we worshiped at Cornerstone Christian Fellowship in Bellevue.

You were the flagship for Prince rackets for so many years. How come you don't use their racket anymore?

I played with the Prince Graphite 110 from when I was ten years old until I was nearly twenty-three years old. That's a long time, especially when you consider all the new rackets that came out in that time or the improvements in racket technology. Nothing I tried, however, felt better than my trusty Prince Graphite.

Then I switched to a Longbody Prince racket at the start of 1994—a story I told in chapter 7. Notwithstanding the wizardry provided by my racket technician, Warren Bosworth, who prepares the frames to my specifications, I recently decided to move on. I started playing with the Babalot racket in 2001. I like the frame, and I feel that it's helping me excel on the court at this stage of my career.

What about your Reebok clothes and shoes?

Reebok still gives me whatever I need, and our very long-term endorsement relationship continues to this day. Lately, I've been wearing some collarless shirts from Reebok. There's a rule against wearing T-shirts in your matches, but we convinced the ATP that my collarless shirts were not T-shirts.

What are those things around your ankles?

They are Kallassy ankle braces, which I wear to prevent me from turning an ankle. They have been a tremendous safeguard for me ever since I sprained my ankle seriously in 1991.

How do you deal with jet lag?

Dealing with changing time zones and lost days and cramped airplanes and sleepless nights is something the public never sees, but it's sure been part of my life. Jet lag doesn't get easier with the years, although I've found what works best for me. If I fly from the States to Europe, I usually arrive in the late morning, so I hit the ground running and try to stay up until the evening. Then I fall into my bed exhausted enough to sleep for eight to ten hours. When I fly to Asia or Australia, I arrive a weary ten to fourteen hours later. It's usually the end of the day or nighttime, so I can go to the hotel room and sleep.

Whenever I travel to another continent by flying overnight or following the sun for mind-numbing hours on end, I know that my body desperately needs rest to perform to its highest ability. I don't take anything like sleeping pills or melatonin or drink a capful of NyQuil. I prefer to let my body deal with jet lag naturally.

Do you have any other hobbies besides fishing?

Playing golf! Seriously, I've become hooked on the game since I took it up during my Christmas break in 2000. I was a real duffer when I started, but now I'm able to score in the 80s on a consistent basis. Carl likes to play as well, so it's fun to see who can hit closest to the pin. Carl's a better player—he's been shooting in the 70s. Frankly, I see myself playing a lot of golf in the future, although I'm only able to play a round here and there with all the traveling I do. But that doesn't keep me from occasionally bringing my clubs along.

Another pastime I enjoy is singing. In Mercer Island, I used to drop by my church on Monday night and sing with the worship band as they practiced for the following Sunday. I know it's hard to picture me up on a stage with a microphone in hand, but I was raised by two parents who love to sing, so their love of music must have rubbed off on me.

Someone must have heard that I enjoy singing because Sony Records approached me in 1997 about cutting an album, mainly for my fans in Asia since I would sing in English *and* Chinese. When I expressed some interest—as long as I could do a Christian song or two—Sony put me through some voice lessons to see if I could actually carry a tune. I met with a voice coach on a few occasions, including once at my house in

Henderson. After spending two hours singing with me, the voice coach, who had worked with Mariah Carey, among others, told Sony that she thought it was *possible* that I had enough singing talent to pull off an album.

"But you have to continue with your voice lessons," said the coach after her final visit.

"Does singing in the shower count?" I asked. "How about singing in the car?"

She smiled. "No, singing in the shower doesn't count," she said. The next step was for me to warble a few songs in a recording studio. We worked it out so that I visited a studio in Taiwan, and after a day or so of laying down some voice tracks—and singing the same line over and over—it really became clear to me that singing was a lot of work. You don't show up in a studio, sing a few songs, and leave. When I saw how time-consuming and difficult singing and pulling an entire album together could be, I started having second thoughts.

Since I don't like to venture into anything halfway, I passed on the project, deciding that I wasn't going to quit my day job to pursue a career in music.

How do your fans in Asia generally treat you?

Very well, and they have to be the smartest fans in the world because they seem to find out which hotel I'm staying in that week, even if it's not the official players' hotel. They've sent e-mails to my private e-mail address. They know when I'm in Hong Kong, even if I'm not in Hong Kong to play a tournament. I've never been able to figure out how they find out I'm there, but when I walk out of my hotel, there are dozens of fans waiting in the lobby, holding cameras and autograph books. I have gotten to know more than a few of them, including four special fans whose names are Haily, Winky, Vicki, and Emma, and every year since I can remember, they have greeted me at the Hong Kong airport upon my arrival.

The four young women are in their mid-twenties, which means that they must have had a puppy love crush on me when they were in middle school. "We're getting kind of old for this," one of them said to me on my last trip, and we all laughed.

In Japan, there's a young woman named Mieko who always sends me a note, wishing me well. Meiko has popped up at the Australian Open and the French Open to see me play. I guess she loves tennis.

What's your favorite food?

Anything Chinese, but to be more specific, I love *sui gao*, or dumplings. It's hard for me to turn down a serving of beef noodle soup or tofu. I love my mom's cooking the best—if I don't have Chinese food regularly, I feel like I'm missing out. I can eat a lot for someone my size. In fact, I can eat four big meals a day and never gain an ounce.

Besides the Grand Slams, what are your favorite tournaments?

There is only one non–Grand Slam tournament that I've played every year during my long career—Memphis. I like Memphis for two reasons: the tournament director is a great guy named Tommy Buford, and the tournament almost always falls on my birthday, February 22. If I happen to be in the tournament on my birthday, Tommy arranges for a birthday cake to be wheeled out to the court following my match. Then I have the annual pleasure of standing there embarrassed while three thousand people sing, "Happy Birthday, dear Michael . . ."

This indoor tournament is held at the Racquet Club of Memphis, which is one of the coziest venues on tours, allowing the players to interact with the fans. The fans practically sit right on top of you, but they have always been kind and warm to me, and I've made great friends with the people working the tournament. Memphis is where I first learned the meaning of the phrase "Southern hospitality."

What's the most embarrassing thing that's ever happened to you?

That's a hard question to answer because there have been so many, but one stands out, and it happened in Memphis. Whenever I travel and check into a hotel, I do not register as "Michael Chang" at the front lobby; to do so would invite phone calls to my room around the clock and I would never get any sleep—or enjoy any privacy.

One year at the Memphis tournament, I checked into the players' hotel as "Christian Brothers." A clever alias, wouldn't you agree? Anyway, someone—my guess is probably a female employee who worked at the hotel—wrote down my credit card number, called Frederick's of Hollywood and Victoria's Secret, ordered a few sexy negligees and other items, and asked for the hot stuff to be shipped to Christian Brothers in care of the Racquet Club of Memphis.

Well, the interesting packages arrived about a week after the tournament was over, and Tommy Buford, who knew my alias, opened the boxes, curious why these types of stores would be sending something my way long after the tournament was finished.

When Tommy called me later that day, I could tell that he was a bit uncomfortable. "Ah, Michael, did your sister-in-law, ah, by any chance order some merchandise from Frederick's of Hollywood and Victoria's Secret and have it shipped to the club?"

"No, Tommy. That doesn't sound like Diana."

"Whew," said Tommy. "You won't believe this stuff, and they are all in 'plus' sizes."

"Plus sizes?"

"Ah, you know, size sixteen."

This was getting really embarrassing.

"Tommy, I think somebody got a hold of my credit card," I offered. "I'm going to have to check it out."

That's what happened all right—someone used my credit card number and ordered a box of frilly undergarments to be sent to Memphis. I canceled my credit card, of course, and quickly received a new one.

That wasn't the first time someone had gotten a hold of my credit card number. I remember another time when I received a phone call from my credit card company. The representative said, "Mr. Chang, we notice that you have had some strange charges to your card. Were you in Reno in the last few days?"

"No, I've been here in Seattle."

"Well, someone in Reno was making five-thousand-dollar cash advances with your credit card."

My sister-in-law, Diana, when she's not ordering from Frederick's of Hollywood (just a joke!), is my accountant. She goes through my card charges *very* closely and is always on the lookout for something out of the ordinary.

Since you wear contacts, have you ever tried to play with glasses?

My eyesight is not 20/20, so I must wear contacts when I play. I do wear glasses on long plane flights or at night. I don't wear them that much, however. When I do wear glasses for an extended time, my eyes get tired.

As for contacts, I've been wearing them for nearly fourteen years, so it takes me two seconds to put them in or take them out. I put on my Acuvue 2 contacts in the morning and take them out in the evening. I travel with two or three boxes of one-day contact lenses, but I treat them like extended wear. I wear them until the lenses start getting protein deposits.

After Wimbledon in 1992, I played the following week in Gstaad, Switzerland. The Alpine setting, blue skies, gingerbread chalets, and Swiss chocolate are wonderful, but being high in the Swiss Alps caused tons of protein deposits to form on my contact lenses. My eyes became very red—as if I had been crying nonstop for two hours.

So for the first—and last—time in my life, I tried to play a match wearing glasses. It was just a doubles match with Carl against Fabrice Santoro and Amos Mansdorf, a twilight affair that started at 6 P.M. in the sunlit Alps.

As we started the match, I asked Carl, "How come there are clouds in the sky?"

"What clouds?"

Then Carl saw the problem—fog on my glasses, and he started laughing. "I think I know your problem," he said.

The next day, I switched to thinner daily-wear contacts. My days of seeing clouds on sunny days are over.

How many autographs have you signed in your life?

I'm getting writer's cramp just thinking about your question. Let's see. When I'm in the public eye at a tournament or traveling in a city, I probably sign 50 to 100 autographs a day. If you figure that happens 200 days a year, I have conservatively signed 10,000 to 20,000 autographs a year since 1989. That means I've probably signed my name around 200,000 times.

When I first started signing autographs, I signed them *God Loves You! MChang.* I thought that would introduce the Lord to people who haven't heard of Him. Then something happened to change my mind. A young girl approached me in Kuala Lumpur when I was playing a tournament in Malaysia and asked me for an autograph. This probably happened in 1991.

I obliged her, and then she stared at the autograph. "I think it's great that you add 'God Loves You,' but there are many people who don't know which God you're referring to."

The young girl was right. Ever since then, I have signed my autographs *Jesus Loves You! MChang*.

I'll tell you something about being on the other end of autograph requests: I always hear when someone says thank you, and it's always appreciated.

You've been interviewed thousands of times. Do any writers stand out to you?

Bud Collins has always been fair, and he has written nice things about me. I've always made it a point to say hello and spend some time with him. I grew up listening to Bud do the color commentary with Dick Enberg at the French Open and Wimbledon. He's clearly the dean of today's tennis writers and someone I highly respect.

Another writer I enjoyed reading is the late *Los Angeles Times* sports columnist Jim Murray. He must have written six or seven columns about me over the years. (I've included one in the next chapter.) I didn't get to know him well personally, but he was very professional in the way he approached his craft whenever he interviewed me. I found it easy to trust him as a journalist.

After being interviewed thousands of times, I can tell you this: I can usually tell what direction the story is heading by the questions they ask or by what they are trying to get me to say. It's sometimes very obvious when someone wants to write a negative story. I guess everyone has his or her own way of operating.

Who do you like as a tennis commentator?

It's seems like every time you turn on a Grand Slam tennis tournament, John McEnroe is offering commentary. John does a fine job and can be witty at times. All in all, I prefer listening to commentators who aren't former tennis players—people like Dick Enberg and Ted Robinson. Bud Collins has a great sense of the history of the game. I'm also a fan of Mary Carillo, who uses colorful and descriptive language when she commentates. Plus, it is always nice to have such people as Mary and Bud want to see you do well on top of everything else.

Do you speak Chinese?

Actually, the question should be: Do you speak Mandarin? The answer is yes and no. Mom and Dad originally spoke nothing but Mandarin to Carl and me during our toddler years, but as Carl started going to elementary school (when I was three years old), they started speaking more English to us.

At the time, it was just easier for them since our schoolwork was in English—it seemed that virtually our whole lives were in English. Like many immigrant families, they wanted us to become native speakers because we were part of the great American melting pot.

Having said that, I *have* learned to speak some Mandarin. I call it "get-by" Mandarin: I can get by when I go shopping in Hong Kong or Shanghai, chat with people I meet, exchange pleasantries, and carry on short conversations. If the conversation requires more depth, I can get lost. Mandarin is a difficult language for people with English as their mother tongue.

Each time I travel to China, however, my Mandarin improves. I return home with greater proficiency and a bigger vocabulary. I've even made short public speeches when handed a microphone, like the one following my win at the Heineken Open in Shanghai.

I will close with this thought: I would love to speak Mandarin fluently some day, and with a little practice, I believe it's possible. It's something I would definitely want for my children because it's all about heritage.

Why have you not played much doubles in your career?

I would have loved to play more doubles, but with the way the Grand Slams and most tournaments are set up, you won't see the top players committing to much doubles play, if any. That's the unfortunate part because I don't mind playing doubles.

But here's the situation: as long as the Grand Slam events are best-of-five sets—and I don't see that ever changing—it's too demanding physically to play singles *and* doubles if you've got a realistic chance of getting into the second week. Your singles game suffers, and you'll be playing against top players who are more rested than you are. Remember: careers are made in the Grand Slams, when the sporting world sits up and takes notice of these historic tournaments.

If you're playing in a smaller tournament, doubles are often scheduled as the last matches of the day. For indoor tournaments, this sometimes means a 10 P.M. start on an evening when you need to rest for your singles match the next day. Then you can run into funny scheduling when matches get rained out. Wimbledon is strange. I've had guys tell me that they played their first rounds of doubles on Tuesday and their second rounds on Wednesday—eight days later! That's what rain and a backlog of matches will do to a major outdoor tournament.

I've heard that you are really famous in Asia. Is that true?

Now my face is turning red. You may have read that I was the "Michael Jordan of Asia" or that I would not walk down a Hong Kong sidewalk without a police escort. I don't know about the former, but regarding the latter, there were indeed occasions when I could not leave my Hong Kong hotel without a security detail. There's no doubt that I have special fans throughout Japan, Hong Kong, China, Taiwan, Singapore, and Malaysia because of my Asian descent.

Have you ever participated in any evangelistic events, like the Billy Graham Crusades?

I have never participated in any large stadium events, but I did tape my testimony for the Billy Graham Evangelistic Association, which became part of a worldwide event in 1995. In March of that year, Dr. Graham traveled to San Juan, Puerto Rico, for a crusade at Hiram Bithorn Stadium. Next door to the stadium, a huge indoor arena housed a dazzling array of technical equipment that transmitted the crusade via satellite to venues in 185 countries and territories.

Skilled interpreters in booths at the indoor arena translated Dr. Graham's message into forty-eight languages. My taped segment was part of the Mandarin language version that was broadcast to the Chinese-speaking world, as were segments by Chinese Christian musical groups.

I have appeared in person at several youth evangelistic events, including the 1997 DC/LA Youth for Christ event that drew tens of thousands of teens.

How often do you have to restring your rackets?

When I play on clay with natural gut strings, the best I can hope for is twenty to thirty minutes of playing time before one of my strings snaps in two. I go through around ten string jobs a day—which means that the stringers at the tournament sites know that I will be a frequent visitor. The gritty clay residue gets on the string and practically saws the gut in two. Since I constantly break strings every thirty minutes or so, Carl is on a fire drill as he shuttles broken string jobs back and forth to the tournament stringer.

How many miles a year do you fly?

A lot! I'm a United Premier and Delta SkyMiles member, and these days I do most of my flying on United and Delta out of Sea-Tac. All in all, I would say that I rack up more than one hundred thousand miles per year on each airline. Like many folks, I receive United and Delta mileage when I make credit card purchases, which dumps even more miles into my accounts. Those miles can come in handy.

A few months before my brother's wedding in the Mission Viejo area, my mother said to me, "Michael, you have a lot of miles. Carl and Diana have invited family members from New York, including my parents. Obviously, if we could use your miles, they wouldn't have to pay for their trip."

What son can refuse his mom? I was more than happy to fly out seven family members from New York City for the wedding.

Are you a night owl or a morning person?

Definitely a morning person. I like to get up early and see what the day has to bring.

What do you like to read?

I like to read Christian books, especially anything written by Max Lucado. He's a wonderful storyteller, and many of his books are a collection of short stories. I often return to authors that I like and know. I usually won't pick up someone's book unless I get a recommendation from a good friend or someone I know from church.

Another favorite author is Charles Stanley, a pastor in the Atlanta area. His *In Touch* program can often be found on Sunday morning television. If I'm flipping through the channels, I always stop if I come across his program. Dr. Stanley also has tons of tapes, and I've ordered many of his teaching series.

Do you watch much TV?

When I'm on the road, I like watching CNN to catch up on the news happening back in the States and elsewhere. CNN is piped into just about every major hotel in the world.

When I'm home, however, I don't watch so much TV. I used to watch cartoons and sitcoms when I was very young, but I've weaned myself from that stuff. And you know what? I don't miss it at all.

Has anyone tried to get you off your game when you're playing a match?

Sure, all the time! It's called gamesmanship when your opponent tries to disrupt your concentration, and gamesmanship has cost me a few matches over the years. Let me give you an example. I was playing this guy—you'd recognize his name—and it was my serve. I bounced the ball twice and when I looked up, he put his arm up to signal that he was not ready. Tennis is a game of pacing, a game of rhythm, so when an opponent disrupts your rhythm, it can throw your game off.

I had played this guy several times before, so I knew what he was doing. This time when he interrupted my service motion, I did something about it.

I turned to the umpire and asked him to ask my opponent if he was ready. On cue, the umpire turned to my opponent and said, "Are you ready?"

"Yes, sure," said the player, although we both knew the request unnerved him. Advantage Chang.

In tennis, there's an on-court game, and then there's a mind game. Players really do try to get inside your head.

Will you ever hit an underhand serve again?

I don't think so. The underhand serve against Ivan Lendl in Paris was a special moment. I haven't hit an underhand serve in a real match since, and I doubt I ever will again.

CHAPTER 14

WHAT'S NEXT?

O ne of the first questions I received after winning the French Open in 1989 was "Will there be more Grand Slams in your future, Michael?"

"I don't want to limit myself," I said on that historic day. "I don't want to say, 'Okay, Michael, you've won Roland Garros and that's it.'" Yet, barring something miraculous from God, it's likely that Roland Garros will be the only Grand Slam trophy sitting in a display case at my parents' Coto de Caza home.

Tennis players, when they are fitted for greatness, are measured by the number of Grand Slam titles they collect over their careers. Roland Garros, Wimbledon, the U.S. Open, and the Australian Open are the Big Four. Win one of those, and you join an elite club of great players.

Yet I never won another Grand Slam. I came close, to be sure. I also came within one match of becoming the No. 1 player in the world.

So how do I feel now that I'm supposed to be reflective on what might have been? I believe I am well-positioned to make this statement: I have experienced an incredibly blessed existence, and I did not need to become No. 1 or win another Grand Slam to live a rich, fulfilling life. I've found the journey I'm on to be much more important than the destination. I know that I am a better person for going through the various tennis trials of the last few years, and with the passage of time, I will come to appreciate the difficulties more because they refined my character.

LOOKING INTO THE FUTURE

So what do I see myself doing after my playing days are over? If you had asked me that back in my teenage years, I would have talked about becoming a marine biologist or going back to college. I don't see those things happening. Oh, maybe I'll take a few classes someday, but I don't envision myself returning to school full-time.

I plan to be involved in tennis one way or another, but as of this writing, I'm not sure where the Lord will call me. Obviously, it won't be playing professional tennis tournaments, but I would like to pursue various avenues of ministry. For some reason—my Asian heritage, to be sure—I feel drawn to China. I know I have a great burden for the Chinese people, and I would seriously consider participating in some missionary-type effort to China and other Asian countries. I would like to take advantage of things I've learned over the years and share them with others. I would like to be an encouragement to other Asians and inspire them to do great things on or off the tennis court.

I also see myself getting married and starting a family, and settling down a bit in Mercer Island, as I mentioned in chapter 9. What I don't see happening is sliding into a rocking chair. A couple of weeks of fishing and golf will be fine, but after that, I will want to do something productive with my life.

Some people have asked me whether I'm going to try out some new sports once my playing days are over. Well, I won't be taking up snowboarding or rock climbing. Bungee jumping is out, nor could I jump off a bridge like Patrick Rafter did a couple of years ago. I'll stick to the golf links, and I would be disappointed if my short game didn't get any better.

I don't think I see myself following in Ivan Lendl's spike marks, however. Ivan, who retired from tennis in 1994 with a bad back, jumped into the golf game with great gusto. Ivan is now a golf nut. Through much practice and effort, he has turned himself into a very good player, good enough to win two Celebrity Players Tour (CPT) events. (Funny thing. I heard that Ivan was *more* excited winning a CPT tournament against the likes of baseball's Mike Schmidt and NFL great Jim Brown than some of his big tennis championships.)

When will I know that it's time to exit stage left from tennis? I'm not sure, although I will say that I would like to play another year or two on the tour. I keep thinking something great is still ahead in my tennis career, and that is what inspires me to keep playing.

Besides, who knows what God has planned . . .

MATCH POINT

When you near the end of your professional sports career, people often ask you how you want to be remembered.

That's a tough question to answer. I hope *Holding Serve* has given you an insight into myself, my life, my Christian beliefs, my character, and the importance of my family.

A column written by *Los Angeles Times* sportswriter Jim Murray several months after I won the French Open in 1989 captures me and my tennis career in ways that are uncanny. After all, he wrote this when I was still seventeen years of age, but in many ways, Jim Murray got it right, which is why I am reprinting (with permission) his column below. In many ways, this is how I would like to be remembered:

Los Angeles Times
September 22, 1989

This Kid Isn't Nasty Enough to Become a Tennis Champion
by Jim Murray

You know tennis in this country is in scandalous condition when a couple of guys named Boris and Ivan are playing for our national open title. I can remember when guys named Boris and Ivan would be heavies in a B movie, not headliners at center court.

So, a lot of people were enormously heartened when, for the first time in 34 years, a Yank won the French Open this year. In the process, he made Ivan look terrible and beat up on a guy named Andrei and the obligatory Swede in the process. At the ripe old age of 17.

Right away, Michael Chang became the darling of American tennis, the Yankee Doodle Dandy who is going to lead us back to the glory days of Big Bill Tilden, Donald Budge, Jack Kramer and Arthur Ashe.

Is he?

Nah!

I hate to be a party-pooper, I hate to rain on the parade but I have to tell you, I have checked out young Master Chang and, from what I can see, he has no chance.

Oh, I'm not worried he doesn't have this cannonball serve. Neither did Bobby Riggs nor Vic Seixas and they won Wimbledon and the U.S. Nor am I concerned that he's always playing guys who are bigger, stronger and sometimes faster than he is. That never bothered Bitsy Grant.

No, my concern is, they haven't groomed him in the proper things to become a tennis champion today. Oh, they taught him all the backhand volleys, the lobs in the lights, the drop shots, the forehands down the line.

But they have to teach him racquet-smashing, linesman-bashing, umpire-baiting. He's about 1,000 swear words short of being a great tennis champion.

They've concentrated on all the wrong things. Anyone with an eye in his head could see what it takes to succeed in tennis today. A rotten disposition. A bad temper. A crybaby mentality.

As near as I can see, Michael Chang hasn't perfected any of those techniques. He isn't even a spoiled brat. How in the world is he going to compete at a world-class level until he learns how to intimidate officials, rattle opponents, strain international relations, bully ball-boys, insult the customers, sulk, pout, whine—do all the things we've come to love and expect from a real tennis champion?

I think Master Michael should immediately take to his room, armed with videocassettes of Ilie Nastase, John McEnroe, Jimmy Connors, and take notes. Get a stop-action on the place where John McEnroe describes the England of Lord Tennyson, King Arthur, Richard the Lion Hearted and William Shakespeare as "the pits." Get a shot of Ilie Nastase spitting all over a luckless lady linesperson he's in such a sputtering rage at over an out call. Turn up the sound when some of the better gutter language begins to issue from the mouths of Jimmy Connors and McEnroe. Learn championship tennis the right way.

Look at Michael Chang on court. He just stands there, poker-faced, inscrutable, patient. . . . He's like that silent kid in the schoolyard you never wanted to get in a fight with because you knew he'd fight you for three days if necessary. And you'd have to kill him to win.

Michael Chang is that way. It's all right with him if every match goes four hours. Or five or six. He's as solemn as a funeral. He seldom changes expression. He just stands there and beats the ball back at you, usually in places you least expect to see it.

But watch him when a call goes against him. That's when you know he's got a long way to go. He just bows his head, bounces the ball twice, raises his racket, serves. No outbursts. No shrieks. He never approaches the chair, the neck cords standing out in his throat, his face red, his language X-rated.

When he wins, he thanks God. When he gets time off, he reads the Bible. What kind of a way is that to get ready for Wimbledon? When's the last time anybody with good manners like that got to be No. 1 in this country?

Is there still time for Michael to learn all the little things you have to learn to play big-time tennis, to become the first-class jerk you apparently have to become to succeed on the tennis tour?

Probably not. He doesn't have the background for it. Michael, you see, is not one of your Long Island sons of riches who got into tennis because his yacht sank. Michael was born in Hoboken. Mom and Dad, Betty and Joe Chang, were émigrés to this country. Joe's family left China to escape Mao's revolution in 1948. Betty is the daughter of a Chinese diplomat, born in India.

Temper tantrums do not run in the family. Michael is going to have to learn them. When the family moved to Southern California, Michael got a tennis racket instead of a surfboard because he may be the only guy in his crowd who gets seasick on shore.

"I get sick just running on the beach," he says.

He passed on baseball because he saw a replay of a beaning incident on television one night.

"They kept playing it over and over till it made you sick," he says. "I decided if I was going to get hit by a ball, it would be a tennis ball."

He got so precocious at tennis, he won his first national tournament when he was 12 and his first national junior by the time he was 15. That got him into Wimbledon, where he was the youngest to play there in 60 years.

Michael has had a variety of tennis instructors over the years, but the four he relies on most are Matthew, Mark, Luke and John. None of them counsel throwing the racket, vilifying the umpire, snarling at the press. The religiosity goes back to a family thing.

"My great-grandmother in Taiwan became ill with cancer, and when it was diagnosed as terminal, my grandmother went to a friend who asked her if she had considered consulting Jesus Christ," Michael explains. "She became a Christian, and my great-grandmother's cancer went into remission for 40 years, the rest of her life."

A strong strain of Christianity flows through the Chang family to this day.

"I was bored by it when I was a kid but one day I heard a preacher say the secret of life was locked up in the Bible," Michael says. "I got curious. I found out that everything the Bible tells you to do is the right thing. I made up my mind to be a better person."

The question is, does being a better person make you a worse player?

Michael Chang is top seeded at the Volvo/Los Angeles tournament at the UCLA tennis center this week, which means you can bring the kids and won't have to hold your hands over their ears whenever he misses a shot or a call. If Michael Chang uses the Lord's name, he's praying, not cursing.

Still, American tennis has a reputation to uphold. If Michael can't live up to it, maybe we can just arrange to play some old McEnroe tapes the next Grand Slam he's in. Otherwise, the way Michael plays it, the world might start liking Americans.

• EMBRACING MY HERITAGE AT THE GREAT WALL OF CHINA •

CHAPTER 15

THE LAST LEVEL OF SUCCESS

I've never been asked to speak at the Peter Lowe Success Seminars—those daylong "yes-fests" that feature live appearances from notables such as George and Barbara Bush, Margaret Thatcher, Colin Powell, Larry King, and Joe Montana. The Peter Lowe Success Seminars are very successful events, selling out sixteen-thousand-seat arenas from coast to coast.

The host of the event, Peter Lowe, speaks in the middle of the afternoon on the Five Levels of Success. When he comes to the fifth point of his presentation, Peter states that the last level of success is based on God, "who says that all things are possible for those who believe."

That statement certainly captures the attention of the audience, which is comprised of business people. Peter continues by saying, "For all intents and purposes, my presentation is over, but if you would like to remain for my fourteen-minute 'bonus session' and learn more about how God could fit into your life, please remain in your seats. We will take a one-minute break before we start again."

In a similar vein, *Holding Serve* is over and you don't have to read on. If you would like to stick around and keep reading, however, I would like to tell you more about how God can become part of your life.

What I'm about to say comes directly from my heart. As I have thought about why I became a successful tennis player, I have come to the realization that I can't answer that question because none of us can know the mind of God. Yet I have always held a strong feeling that God granted me a measure of on-court success because that allowed me the chance to tell others about Jesus Christ. That's why I have seen myself as an evangelist with a tennis racket ever since I won the French Open. No, I haven't preached from Court Central, but I've tried to live my life as an example of Christ and to point others toward Him. This is what we call the good news—Jesus Christ came to us as, God as a human, died and was raised from the dead, and opened the door for God's kindness to be poured out on us.

I used to put too much emphasis on winning and losing, but my perspective changed when I became a Christian. He gave me a real sense of peace, especially after I learned that God can touch lives through my wins *and* my losses. No, it hasn't been easy dropping out of the top 10 for the last few years, but I have striven to give God the glory in *whatever* the circumstance. I know that God has had a purpose for everything, and that belief has freed me.

To me, the real meaning of Christianity is having a personal relationship with Jesus. I have found no greater joy than knowing the Lord, and I want you to experience that same joy. I believe God has called me to share His love with you . . . a love that is patient and kind . . . a love that will cause you to desire change . . . a love that will heal your deepest hurts.

It is not my intention to force Christianity down your throat because that is not the way God wants us to come to Him. My purpose is to help you discover a meaningful, exciting, and lasting relationship with Jesus Christ and develop into the person God created you to be. He cares about every little detail of your life and desires to have an intimate relationship with *you*. Psalm 139:13–16 says:

> For you [God] created my inmost being;
>   you knit me together in my mother's womb.
> I praise you because I am fearfully and wonderfully made;
>   your works are wonderful,
>   I know that full well.
> My frame was not hidden from you
>   when I was made in the secret place.
> When I was woven together in the depths of the earth,
>   your eyes saw my unformed body.
> All the days ordained for me
>   were written in your book
>   before one of them came to be.

In the Bible, the "Roman Road" teaches us that everyone has sinned (Rom. 3:23), that the penalty for sin is death (Rom. 6:23), that Jesus Christ died for our sins (Rom. 5:8), and that to be forgiven for our sins, we must believe and confess that Jesus Christ is Lord because salvation comes only through Jesus Christ (Rom. 10:8–10).

If you feel God tugging at your heart, if you want to ask Him into your heart and trust in Him to save you, all you have to do is this:

1. Admit your need to God.

2. Be willing to turn from your sins and change your selfish ways.

3. Believe that Jesus Christ died for you on the cross and rose from the grave.

4. Ask Him to come into your life.

If you're ready to receive Jesus into your life, then pray this prayer with me:

> Dear Jesus, I come to You right now . . . and admit that I am a
> sinner. I repent of my sins against You. I believe that You died on
> the cross for my sins . . . and that You rose again three days later.
> I know that if I believe in You I will have eternal life with You. I
> ask that You forgive me . . . and that You come into my life. Amen.

Did you say that prayer? If so, welcome to the kingdom of God! I know the Lord wants to watch out for you, guide you, teach you, love you, and give you the peace in your life that you've always longed for. Be sure to tell a friend or pastor what you've done.

In closing, I want to thank you for joining me on this life journey that the Lord has me traveling on. I've enjoyed every moment trying to "hold serve" in a manner that would be pleasing to Him. Take care and may God bless you as only He can.

ACKNOWLEDGMENTS

Where do I begin? So many people have been helpful to me over the years. At the risk of overlooking someone deserving, I would like to begin by thanking my brother, Carl, who has been there through thick and thin. Thank you for your love and dedication to helping me become my very best. My sister-in-law, Diana, who has been more of a sister than anything else, has been a wonderful blessing to me. To my grandparents, Ke-Wu and Pey-Fang Chang and Michael and Dorothy Tung, thank you for your precious love and countless hours of prayer for all your loved ones. To my little niece, Katie, your arrival into all our lives couldn't have been more perfect. We praise the Lord for the blessing of you and your smile.

Tom Ross, my longtime agent at Octagon, has done an incredible job managing my career and opening the doors to numerous and exciting opportunities over the years. Kelly Wolf, who works closely with Tom at Octagon, somehow kept me organized with interviews and appearances, among other things, just as long. Thank you both for caring so much for me, and for all your hard work. Dianne Hayes of Reebok has been a faithful friend and supporter. Ken Matsuda, my trainer and good friend for over ten years, has not only kept me in shape, but also has been a great motivator. To my family and friends in Seattle, southern California, New York, Texas, and around the world, thank you for your prayers and support.

As for this book, I enjoyed being paired with my writing "doubles partner," Mike Yorkey, who did a great job incorporating my thoughts and turning them into the volume that you now hold in your hands. I appreciate how Janet Thoma at Thomas Nelson Publishers shepherded the project from start to completion. Christin Ditchfield of Sarasota, Florida, who has written extensively about me for Christian publications, provided us with her treasure trove of interviews and background information. Thanks go to Lynette Winkler of Spiez, Switzerland; Trent and Mary Gaites of Flowery Branch, Georgia; and Nicole Yorkey of Encinitas, California, for reading earlier versions of this manuscript. Editorial assistance was also provided by Per Knuts and Jocelyn Fiene, as well as by Stephan Brun of the French Tennis Federation.

Lastly, to my fans around the world, you have always believed and will continue to believe. That means so much to me. Thank you!